THE BEST POEMS AND POETS OF 2003

The International Library of Poetry

Howard Ely, Editor

The Best Poems and Poets of 2003

Library of Congress
Cataloging in Publication Data

ISBN 0-7951-5245-0

Proudly manufactured in the United States of America by
Watermark Press
One Poetry Plaza
Owings Mills, MD 21117

poetry.COM

FOREWORD

Throughout life, we store information collected from experiences and try in some way to make sense of it. When we are not able to fully understand the things that occur in our lives, we often externalize the information. By doing this, we are afforded a different perspective, thus allowing us to think more clearly about difficult or perplexing events and emotions. Art is one of the ways in which people choose to externalize their thoughts.

Within the arts, modes of expression differ, but poetry is a very powerful tool by which people can share sometimes confusing, sometimes perfectly clear concepts and feelings with others. Intentions can run the gamut as well: The artists may simply want to share something that has touched their lives in some way, or they may want to get help to allay anxiety or uncertainty. The poetry within *The Best Poems and Poets of 2003* is from every point on the spectrum: every topic, every intention, every event or emotion imaginable. Some poems will speak to certain readers more than others, but it is always important to keep in mind that each verse is the voice of a poet, of a mind that needs to make sense of this world, of a heart that feels the effects of every moment in this life, and perhaps of a memory that is striving to surface. Nonetheless, recalling our yesterdays gives birth to our many forms of expression.

Cover art: "Erie Basin Marina Lite" by Norman Wisniewski

Pages in My Mind

Come sit with me
before our life has passed
I need your help
to turn the pages in my mind

We can share precious moments,
moments that will never be forgotten
moments of trying times,
heartaches, love--yes
all precious moments

Turn the pages my love--
see every minute as precious time,
hold my hand, let me lay my head
on your shoulder

Stroll through the pages
of my mind with me, and
when the final page is turned--
kiss me, never let go of my hand

As you leave, I want to know
that one day soon-you will
lift, me to join you and only my
footprints will remain

Mildred G. Henry

Midnight, Winter

Midnight, winter, on a back road,
Headlights sweeping mounds of snow.
Frosted by night, each day they melt
A little. A dark seep of water
That gathers into pools for wind and thaw
And spring to drive away the last remains.
Each mound looming out of the night
Is witness to a lover's final meeting.
A cold, pale, monument to the end,
The beginning of chill separation.
Starkly beside the road each mound
Remembers where a car was parked,
How looks were once exchanged and
How words passed between two people.
It remembers, it feels their passing.
It weeps for lost love's lost intimacy,
Till spring wildflowers return again
And cars pause briefly on their way.

Andrew Burnside

Air Ballet

You stand poised and stately
Atop the pole beside the marina.
Neck stretched and almost on tiptoe,
You launch yourself gracefully,
Wings stretched wide.
Behind you the pole dances wildly,
Belying the gentle energy seemingly exerted,
Gliding gently and smoothly down to sea level.
The smooth sea absorbs you
As you dip to find lunch;
A good meal found,
Return to the pole once more.
Sun drying feathers speedily in gentle breeze;
For one so large, you defy gravity.
In these gentle climes,
A pelican's life seems easy.

Madeline Cameron

Blurry Face

She puts mascara on a blurry face,
Hoping her hand remembers the movements
She can no longer guide with her sight.
She wonders at the years
She's been performing this simple ritual,
Designed to add color and definition to her features
While the natural definition slowly fades.

She reaches out to touch the mirrored image
Softened by age and poor vision,
And wonders where she's gone.
Where's the adventurous girl? The confident young woman?
Have they been masked by career and family concerns?

She finds her glasses and reaches for her lip pencil,
Hoping to accent the twinkle in her eye
With a shy smile.
Hoping to capture herself again.
Hoping those she meets will see in her
What she has trouble seeing for herself,
What she has to take by faith.

Charlene A. Derby

Gypsy

She is gypsy-like, with broken fairy wings
She holds her disenchanted dreams within those empty seas of eyes
And then she cries; she cries like no one cries
She crawls; she claws her way into the light
Every day she lives and dies
While sleeping soundly at the same time
Oh, she closes up her gypsy eyes and flies away
When she awakes, she spreads her tattered wings
And through her screams she tries to sing
A lullaby to keep the night away
And then she cries; she cries like no one cries
She crawls; she claws her way into the light
Every day she lives and dies while sleeping soundly at the same time
Oh, she closes up her gypsy eyes and fades away
As the pain rips through she thinks of you
And whispers little spells until the memory recedes into the shadows
Still she cries; she cries like no one cries
And she burns; she's learned that nothing lasts forever

Emily Jeanne Eppig

Artist's Profile
Armin Wilson
Kennett Square, PA, USA

I was a chemist by profession, but I have written poetry for upwards of forty years. I understand poetry is a hard and mean boss, demanding both logic and values. I avoid the first person singular in my poetry, trying to write about what I see before me. The political and social scene is really a lot of suffering and tragedy that is, fortunately, leavened by comedy. I am never really satisfied with the result. I feel comforted, though, in that even great poets leave only a poem or two that makes us bolt upright.

The World Sees

The cut hay
Awaiting the bailer
Thinks of grass paradise
Sees paradise
A boon for the hurt stalk

The cricket dips its delicate mouth
In the mountain spring and thirsty
Tastes an insect heaven
Sees it clearly before its eyes
A glowing reflection of its soul

The elm leaf
Smells the earth, its grandmother
A parent trying to save it from passing and
Sensing eternity
Sees its parents as it falls

The lowly snake
Hears the sudden step of Man
And knows
Sees
Its Eden confined to the centuries

Armin Wilson

Skittish Bird

The shadow of my pen
brushes the page
but the ink does not
for the skittish bird
visiting my park table
beneath light-swaying branches
that tower only with gentleness
fears anything heavy
heavy and sharp

Kathryn Young

Bishop Wright of Pittsburgh, 1961

A sunny, golden day,
The hill looking down the city steps—-
Once wooden and nail,
Now poured concrete—-
Leading to Spring Garden.

The bishop touched us lightly
At Most Holy Name of Jesus,
And we supposedly entered the universal,
Designated citizens
Before Vatican II.

On the way out,
The bishop stopped to speak with a disheveled working man
Sitting in a front pew.

"How are you? How is your wife?"

The entire procession stood and waited.

What time was then? Whose future followed?
How could we know?

Diana Goodavage

Requiescat

To my sister

I shall lie submerged by the sea tide.
Rhythmic waves, stronger than all desire,
will cover me
and reluctantly recede
from the rocky beach
with a long low moan.
I shall not taste the kiss of salt froth
on broken lips,
nor feel the caress of seaweed
more tantalizing than memory
across blinded eyes.
I shall sink quietly into silent depths.
There, beyond all emotion,
I will not hear
one solitary seagull
cry my requiem.

Mary Velma Graham

Moonlight

Now are the days I think of her so
Restless beside old water
A hand that moves through stale air
To sound the clouds like bells

But she is Shelley's moonlight
Waiting by a wall for darkness
She can only hope and travel
And leave her breath on glass

Jeremy Hall

Untitled

you smoke parliaments
before class to warm up, and
the way you inhale and exhale,
the smoke curls around your lips like music.
somehow you can make
even the worst things beautiful.
you hold the smoldering cigarette
between your slender fingertips
and talk to the kids around you who
seem so much alike, but are so different,
and I think that's why you relate to them.

I can't help but wonder
what problems you try to exhale
along with the smoke.

I look at you and wish
it was me you crave between classes, and
late at night,
my breath going in and out of your lungs
and my fingers that you hold
so carefully
between yours.

Erin Noreen Fenton

for the tired new york lover

new york pulses with energy
forged from soot and steel
tired faces nodding above gray suits
on the subways, humanity so exaggerated, no place to retreat
and you, the nomad,
trudge on, seeing nothing
only the spectre of one great woman,
a queen hovering on the horizon of the past
los angeles pulses with energy,
dreamers in drag
eternally young at any cost
fancy so exaggerated
nothing can be believed
i too am haunted; i am a satellite
and the moon is my only true friend
but i have become my own queen
i will draw down the power to heal you
and wait and see if it is welcomed

McKenna W. Rowe

Artist's Profile
Mustafa Demiri
Marlboro, NJ, USA

I am a writer of children's literature, and I often find solace in the writing of poetry. I wrote this poem in celebration of childhood; the faith and the fantasy that all children possess, the precious ideas that kindle the imagination, and the pure hearts in which our hopes reside. At present, I am in the process of writing a novel for children. I write it with the intention that it will stand as a work complex in structure, lucid in format, and significant in substance. It was the recognition of this poem that re-sharpened my almost blunted purpose. Thanks.

The Knight of the Dandelions

In the polar forges of the King of Yule,
A sword was wrought by elves for him,
And found by him beneath a spruce
In the crystal winter morning dim.

He met the winged heralds of Primavera,
When they came singing into his realms.
He scattered the plumes of the dandelions,
And climbed upon the giant elms.

In the glowing breath of a golden summer,
A rival, fierce, he did espy.
It was a green-scaled hedgerow dragon
On the borders of the emerald rye.

With Yultic blade, he battled it
While the moon did wax and wane,
And forty days hence the battle began,
The hedgerow dragon was slain.

When the fairy lanterns came no more,
And the starlit night sent zephyrs cool,
He slept that night 'neath blushing elm,
And dreamt of his first day at school.

Mustafa Demiri

Artist's Profile
Brian M. Sousa
Wakefield, RI, USA

I graduated from Boston College in 2001, an English major with concentration on creative writing. Although I am currently working on a collection of short stories, I love the lyrical voice poetry gives the writer, the ability to create images and feelings in direct, concise form.

Last Fall

You told me once
that each morning
that you awoke in my bed
you reached over,
gently pulled
my arm over you.

Your back was facing me
as I covered you
and let you return to your dreams—
reconfigured, warm, and whole.

I nodded as if I remembered
when you said this,
staring at the backs of your thighs,
soft and pale in the rusted daylight
falling through the stained windows
of October in Boston.

It all fell apart so quickly,
I never had the chance to tell you
that I never noticed.

I never told you that I was always deeply
asleep,
content to be lost
in some other world
every time you changed me.

Brian M. Sousa

In the Magic of the Night

Moonlit beams on melting mounds,
Starlit scorching fire lights,
Soft dew on dry grounds,
Warm breezes on summer nights.
Laughing, illuminated brooks,
Chirping tree frogs winking madly,
Singing crickets in hidden nooks,
Wind whisping short and sadly.
Feet that move in rhythm with mine,
Softly stealing there and back,
Bare and white they intertwine,
Against the night's velvet black.
I hear your voice so close to me,
Floating on firefly's wings,
So crisp and near, so warmly,
Saying thoughts of secret things.
Here we'll dance 'til sunrise,
And black turns to burning bright,
Just you and me and starlit skies,
And the magic of the night.

Emily Marie du Houx

I Buried

I fold Grandpa's plain white T-shirt,
Wondering if the last time he wore it
He knew it would be the last time he wore it.
Callused fingers mead the cotton.

Yesterday, the rusty forklift
Bearing silver chains
Dangled the cement vault lid
Over Grandpa's sealed coffin, midnight blue.
Steady. Lower. Down. Release.

Silver links clinked across
The bronze crucifix before
Cemetery dirt poured like grain
Into Grandpa's grave
With a mildly dull umph.

My heart no longer beats.
It strikes at my chest,
A pounding quite visible,
Even through the white
Of a plain cotton T-shirt.

Daniel Kenneth Hahn

Only by Night

I know by the words you used to describe the times
we spent together that many dreams have
since disfigured your memory of our homeland. I am
able to hear in your speech the desire and

the torment that have corrupted your remembering.
You seem to imagine slopes, for example,
where none existed, as a way of insisting that you
have become a stranger irrevocably. Try to

think of the distortions as glassblowers' warps: Memory
has retained the same light as ever, but it has
distended the dimensions of cherished and forlorn objects.

Go back, if you must, but only by night. Then
the redress to your memory will be less severe than if
you returned in the clear and cruel light of day.

Carl Andrew Wiener

The Same

He carries letters
In his pockets
Memories of what was
Reminders of what will never be
He tells himself
"She's changed"
But inside he knows
The problem is
That he has stayed the same

Colleen Nicole Fardoe

Cloy

There is too much
lavender in
the cupboard.

Received from a
lady who once
amused

but now leaves me
shaking my limbs
and growling

like a dog.

That she once gave
too much lavender
doesn't count

in her favour.

Evie Anderson

Sand

In this world of convenience
we scarcely notice our lives
absorbed through the screen

Soft electric lights
burn shadows in the walls
Time slips from our hands
like fallen sand

While beyond the shades
the world spins outside
encircling the gloom
Time stands still
as we grow old

Eric Lundy

You Have Not and Yet . . .

I have been jaded by legacies.
I have seen the uneven darkness
Creep in contemplation with a rising sun.
I have cried tears
As dry as sands or bleached bones.
I have watched justice fall at its own hands.
I have known what fear lies will take
And risen in the wound and cried
"I am ready!"
When all around are manifest deaths
Which gawk with orb-less eyes.
You have not and yet;
You speak to me of passion and of love,
Caress my ears with soft familiars,
Give me dreams of sunsets and a tear that falls for grace,
And cried for all your newness,
"I am here and will not leave you to this death!"

Ira W. Claxton

A Deeper Depth

Levitating in life at the close of the day
Holds my humanity in silent renewal
Searing my sins to the surface

Breathing without brevity, the welcome release
Sinking to serenity, and back again
Undeserved, but unable to object

Gripping the gravity for the first time
Quite like quantifying the eternities
Replenishing the reason in reality

Cleansing in classic form, purification
Time is trivial, at least for now
Without the worries to weigh

Cyrano De Bergerac

Love Drying on the Trapeze

We falter alone,
I stay beside you, listening as
you share my oxygen in the silence;
like thunder, it rolls.

Rising, and falling, thumping and pulsing,
the rhythms of your heart held to my ear,
I press into your chest,
vibrations of sleep rise;
I am alone, you faltered.
next time,
I will falter, you'll be alone.

And when the trapeze stops its swinging,
I'll pick up the broken pieces on the floor.

We faltered, gambled, lost, naught gaining,
your heartbeat in my ear to echo,
mingled with the salt of my tears staining
your shirt, mixing in the morning dew.

Wake up, and you'll never know it,
but honey, we missed again.

Erica Lynn Moffatt

silent

i remember the silence in between
when a glistening bead dropped from my brow and entered your eye
you smiled as you winked
and just then i wanted to tell you how much
but the words got stuck in my throat
and the silence remained

Andrew Agostino

Artist's Profile

Victoria Mary Rashid
Providence, RI, USA

Also referred to as the Renaissance by the locals, presents a perfect blank canvas, so to speak. There's been many changes in this atmosphere of growth; not all, however, are viewed as positive. So I wrote this poem in the true spirit of rebuttal. You see, while I love the hopeful future our Renaissance presents, I'm seeing very little evidence of this. I'm also wondering the image we foster when our leaders cut educational programs and raise residential taxes. Do we simply wish to feed the corporate giant, and are we looking to perpetuate this drastic image?

The Inner-City Recluse

The garden of stale cinder has been overwrought by design,
plagued by thickly crusted pebbles,
lacking in the staples of society's bread.

Feral cats hunt fattened rodents with greasy whiskers,
children pause only a moment from play.
Humanity withdraws her tethered hand.

Crabgrass peeks through small cracks in narrow sidewalks.
Discarded bottles scent the air with old ale.
Ants lap up remnants of barley.

A faded blue Pinto with patches of rust offers her shelter.
A tenant pants in the noontime heat
while a flea battles a mite for old pit hide.
Outsiders take their part of refuse and public assistance,
speaking new languages, smiling broadly.
Everything is redundantly ironic.

Victoria Mary Rashid

Artist's Profile
Michelle Laura Thoeny
Pleasanton, CA, USA

I am an English major with a creative writing option at California State University, Hayward. After graduation I plan to write fiction for a living.

Piano Lesson

Perched up on telephone books, I struggled
to reach the pedals, white spotted with black.
Middle C was drowning. I was all thumbs
playing Rachmaninoff heavy-handed,
Fingers contorted to outstretched octaves;
I watched black blur into infinity.
Fat cats were drowsy in my theory-caused
mind. Stuccoed walls cringed, rumbling vibrations.
Mentor observed while tapping time with a
rusty pencil on my mahogany
Yamaha. Sighing, she stood to amend
and sat tandem, slender fingers arcing
preludes, sonatas, ballads, and nocturnes
every Tuesday afternoon at four.

Michelle Laura Thoeny

Obliteration

Robert, my chauffeur,
was asked by his little one:
"What does the gleaming cross
around your neck mean?"

Robert, the windbag,
launched with fervor into
Herrod's tyranny, the
Lord's advent,
frankincense and myrrh,
Judas, the Last Supper,
and the Crucifixion.

The little one gazed in awe
And merely said:
"To me it looks like
the 'I' has been crossed!"

Harkara Rajendra Prasad

Western Springs, Summertime

I ride beneath your wing of fluff and
hard-pithed feather stems
Boat within boat, strapped life-vessel tight
Your head turns in gentle directions
to preen furred filaments
and filter reed
for elver and fingerling
With black-specked beak of crimson blood
you kill and calm
I, the parasite—
am soothed and helpless
Locked together—Russian doll
we create a river of twisted deltas
in the flat varnished lake-slick
Oar-feet paddle and twist
I feel and learn from sliding hip sockets
and occasional visits from
your floppy thalidomide leg of pink
that scuffles and brushes
as it hoists to rest

Jennifer Haslam

Final Song

I laugh at Death every time I sing,
He frowns and bares his jaw,
I sing louder.
For twenty, forty, eighty years.
Death still resides in me,
He might tap my sternum,
Grace my spine,
As he makes love to mortality.

In life,
I am careless and I couldn't care less
If Death is my final spectator.
He is my last dream—my only,
Honest salvation.
Bring Death in, only to deny him.

This is not goodbye,
Hear me as I sing:

Only believers in Death will die.

Daniel Stathis Barker

Ship of Indifference

When I wake in light hours the world moves on
Its dreary beat instilling a slow progression
Of life without meaning.
I have been left in its wake
With an empty head
To walk in a cacophony of twilight's myriad images.
I watched my dreams sink in peril
From ships of indifference, unceremonious.
Why me, why so frail?
Yet I see all of Man's gems as coal;
All his moments of genius,
Like a three-year-old's joy with paint and paper,
Grubby fingers on grown-ups' palettes,
Chiding and playing charades.
This is my home now, inconsistency bearing down on me;
Holding the wire between the barbs,
Threading my silk net among the thorns,
Treading eggshells on acid-washed floors,
Waiting for the rains to wash me away.

Michael Steele Taylor

Nexus Point

The primal forces gather,
each to their own,
in preparation
for the final confrontation.
The momentum,
building in cycles as old
as the planet itself,
approaches critical,
yet we still fail
to even notice.
Absorbed by ourselves,
crowded deep into our egos,
we search for answers,
missing the point,
that, after all,
we simply
must love
to erase hate.

Walter "Pat" Patrick Love

My New Suit

I can still feel the rough, sandy, bricks
under my fingers as I climbed
up to the second story walkway
where sat Grandpa's castle.
I crept unnoticed past his window,
pausing by the door in anticipation
of the eminent beard-burn and sack of pennies,
for candy down at the dime store.
I paused briefly at the door,
to dust off my brand-new suit,
and straighten the clip-on bow tie;
after all, Grandpa had never seen my suit.
But Grandpa's whiskers got shaved that day,
the day I made my climb.
Anxiously anticipating and nervously waiting
and as for that dark, blue, velvet suit . . .
well, Grandpa never got the pleasure
of untucking my new white button-down,
or spewing his Rolling Rock laughter
as he chinned my belly red.

Tim S. McAuley

Artist's Profile
M. D. Harrison
Claremont, VA, USA

My occupation as a magistrate and a historian enables me to seek the characteristics which appear in today's society just as in past eras. My poetry expresses the need to recall and connect with our past.

The Forgotten Stone

I strolled one misty morning across a battleground
Where the Blue fought the Gray for the cause of each.
The grass was neatly clipped, the statues on their mound,
The cannon shining with dew, the signs placed to teach.

As I walked slowly upon this hallowed ground and park,
I came to a wooded stand of oak, elm, and pine.
Before me was a faint trail having few signs or even a mark,
A tiny path that beckoned me to follow it on the old line.

A mile or more I tromped, curiously seeking the unknown,
Until I came to an ancient oak more dead than alive.
Here my eyes beheld a partially buried and weathered stone
Leaning against the tree, seemingly attempting to survive.

The stone had such an odd shape, so on my knees I went down.
I began to scratch and brush away the moss, dust, and debris.
Then I saw it: A roughly chiseled name on its crown,
With the faded letters of "U. S." marked barely so as to see.

I stood up in awe and to honor this man who had so little sign,
For no other graves appeared in sight of he who was so alone.
Then I saluted and wandered off to ponder in my weary mind
How this soldier came to lie under the worn, forgotten stone.

M. D. Harrison

Grandpa

I remember running through the garden with you,
picking the best strawberries and carving a zucchini boat out of a
world record zucchini
and sitting on the porch as we listened
to the soaring jets and trilling birds
and walking to the park and
you
polishing the rocks from the river
until they shone.

I remember the fear
when I saw the countless bottles of pills
and the giant machine to clean
your kidneys.

I remember the fear,

and how it hurt so bad when I lost you.

Chelsea Sphinx Brothers

cancer
for my mandy

dawn lights my cigarette
i lie here and wait for her
i feel the scent of her soap
as it washes under the door
i roll last night's quiet sighs between
my fingers
she
is
my faithlessness
what dream does she see
slide into the spiraling drain
locks of hair fall into the stream
i hear her bite her lip as she
clicks her brittle knuckles against time
my shadow
i paint my door with lamb's blood
i pray that she doesn't passover

leah knight

Artist's Profile
Tjuanda Anderson
Detroit, MI, USA

This poem barely skims the surface of the wonderful, vivacious woman that my mother was before being stricken and finally succumbing to a terminal illness. It was written for my sister, Yolanda and my daughter, Shanna, so that remembering the joy of her smile would only be a poem away. I've been writing everything from creative grocery lists to full-length novels for as long as I can remember. My husband, Harry, has finally convinced me to share these scribbles with the rest of the world. I am currently working on a romance novel to submit to Harlequin Romances.

Light As a Feather

There was a 1969 photo of you
smiling with a face I didn't recognize
on a body that seemed too full and wanton.
I hadn't remembered that your skin gleamed
like polished mahogany, or that you loved to
wear opera-length satin gloves (believing it
to be the epitome of high fashion).
That hot night in late August, when you sat
wide-legged, feet splayed apart with a pot of
snapped green beans settled between your
thighs and laughing like a loon at the sheer
joy of a thunderstorm. . . .
That memory had simply flown from existence.
For so long . . .
there had been only the image
of your tiny, helpless body
cradled against my breast . . .
as I must have been once comforted at your own.

Tjuanda Anderson

Artist's Profile
Donna Tuttle
Appleton, WI, USA

God gives eternal life to those whose lives have no sin. But not one person can ever meet this requirement. God knows this, and He loves you so much that He sent His Son, Jesus, to erase our sins forever. The funny thing is that God will not force eternal life upon you if you do not want it. You must first repent the things you know you've done wrong, and ask Jesus to forgive you for them. Jesus is faithful and true; He will forgive you when you ask Him to. Jesus will never leave you or forsake you. Friend, eternal life is yours, just ask for it!

Our Coffee Table

We built a coffee table, you and me.
Thirty plus years in construction, we built with care.
We made the foundation sure and strong. Nothing's wrong.
Forever molding it to our needs. It's respect.
We used it well: Pumpkin pie, soda and life-changing stories.
The years go by fast, we etched in our marks
Of spots, stains, and scratches. Regardless, who sees a defect?

Why we threw that coffee table down the river that day, who can say?
The river had its way, the remains busted and broken.
Comfort ruined now, needs great repair.
Coziness gone, no longer fits us.
Awkward and useless, you thought we should hide it away.
Ever again, can it see the light of day?

How I miss our coffee table.
Nothing else around, nothing compares; our design was priceless.
Foundation, is it strong?
Repairs will be costly: Time, commitment, and sacrifices.
Let's bring it out, you and me; we'll fix her.

Donna Tuttle

Heron

He blends almost fully
into the pull of tide, a long
stretch of neck arched above folded wings.
He seems to glide backward
in meditation

with all the patience and ease
of Jesus fishing for breakfast at dawn.
His gaze piercing the surface, he is lost
in the ripple of migrating waters
only to appear again, stark

as a bone of driftwood against a dark eddy.
In this moment he strikes with such grace
that I desire to imagine his prey
doesn't suffer; that it comes to him, willing
to die so beautifully.

Ronda Kay Broatch

The Bricklayer

I am a layer of bricks.
Strong hands pile strong stones,
piling, piling—layer on layer.
My bricks are strong, like my hands,
red like my blood,
dense like my mind,
heavy like my heart.
I am a layer of bricks.
Thick cement binds these layers,
gooey, mushy—layer on layer.
My cement is fast drying, like my tears,
pasty like my skin,
rough like my conscience,
hard like my soul.
I am a layer of bricks.
Built to fit my pattern, to wear for my cape,
clinging close now, layer on layer,
piling, piling, piling.
This shroud is my world, a case for the quill.

Lori Anne Whitaker

Alone on a Bridge

It seems cruel
to be poor in autumn,

to stand alone on a bridge
feeling at the same time

divided and connected
by a river banked

in golden trees
burdened with change.

Julie L. Hobson

Gifts

Words fall from Grandma's apron,
Worn calico, ginger-apple dusty,
Damp with child's tears.
When I dream of her . . .
Quiet story voice, Finnish-tinged,
Raising only at the blue jay stealing
Bread crumbs from the sparrow.
I am ten . . .
"Sleeping" by her window
Where she sits in tired moonlight
Pulling hairpins from a bun
So joyous, frce . . .
We hold hands,
Slow walk past the daisies to the berries
Blue-ripe, dew-wet,
Filling baskets in the sun.
I write love on this space of paper,
Bearing down hard, like Grandma did,
To give my mother life,
Then me.

Marlene L Settanni

Weight

Held down by six feet of earth
Nails and hickory, cedar and incense
Salty air wafts across a silent field
Stones strewn all about
The memories are still alive

Guilty pleasures
Memories of a time
When sin was unknown
Dreams and hopes
Never were lost before

The sun dies
The moon is reborn
All is bathed in silver
Heavenly beams of light fall
All around this hallowed place
Where all gather together
And rest, with never a thought
Of waking again

Cameron Craft Lincoln

Wisp of Mind

I drowse in ether.
Wisps of genius flutter within reach
but hands are paws,
unclutchable motes,
sand, rain.
The bony earth leans on me.
It whispers fleeting
secrets to my drum,
deaf ears. Fallen leaf,
earth, water.
Nights of Babylon—
wine glass laughter,
geese-babbling fools see eyes as moons
while lips hide sneers,
wind, smoke.
The crow minces,
round eye cocked wide to peck at a dream.
Only stones and hoopla,
the worm is Buddha,
sing, dance.

Anthony Pounders

Artist's Profile
William T. Neal
Richmond, VA, USA

She was my child bride-to-be (my soul mate). I was out of the U.S. Air Force in Virginia. She was in Texas awaiting graduation in June so we could marry in July. This poem was part of a letter I wrote to her that she saved all of these years. We were happily married for 46 ½ years. She was so loved by so many and I miss her so.

November, 1953

The night and I
And thoughts of you
Walk hand in clutching hand
Down shadow-silent streets;
The absolute last night of fall.

And fallen leaves, all brown and crisply dead,
Not as before, (with vivid hues illuminating
Gaily swirling pools)
Must dance together now
Awaiting cold eternity.

Oh! The fogful night so lone and soft
But in the distance
So full of you
That I should almost kneel beside the altar-curb
And pray appreciation.

William T. Neal

New Year's Eve, Putah Creek

Somehow my body knew to come here.
On the eve of a thirty-second year always go down
the way a turtle does; surrender without sinking.
Behind me the road croaks, black oaks move in fog
down to banks crooked with logs, heavy with lichen.
Halfway across the river a pointed silk and whiskery face
twitches, the otter revealed by a water trail,
the length of his thick tail wider than a snake.

Beneath a stream of bubbles he disappears, pops up, closer.
Half the ardor of the world could settle in that lithesome body,
made for cruising streams slimy with winter bacteria.
Hooded mergansers, buffleheads—their white helmets distinct
against the ordinary colorings of other divers—
scatter the surface on an updraft.

Even a torn mind knows to follow the curiosity of water,
to stand still as wet willows and shed the weightiest bark.

Alexandra Hilary Gordon

Man

A lone man sits under a tree.
The wind blows the leaves like crumpled paper.
He sits and wonders, "How come? Why?"

His back against the bark,
too rough for sandpaper.
An ant crawls by, silent as the dark.

The man, wondering what he did wrong,
Wallows in his pity.
He starts to hum a song.

Sweet notes of music fill the air.
The ant comes closer still.
The man gets up, feeling better, seemingly without a care.

An uplifted step he takes.
The ant, unseen, is crushed.
As easy as life comes, it goes.

Samuel Tyler Cruise

One-Room Apartments

Slapped back
Cracked wide open
Until only its insides can be seen.
Dark and ominous
Stretched so tight
That white light is only a faint memory.
Too far away
To penetrate
Concrete walls
Or to warm cold stairs.
Too light-handed
To break the crease
In between
Doorways.
The way a lone meal
Seems to be
An over-focused photograph
Or a telephone's quiet
Is only heightened
By the fact that it never seems to ring.

Steven Daniels

Southampton August

Outside fields
of hay cry reap
odoring sensuous pods
of fuzz and seed
Cows stand guard
with vacant stare
while boys pursue
new mischief
Corncobs wane
on summer breezes
though nearby horses
mind only their flies
Inside goes
the daily business
of household wash
and cooking smells
Clocks stand still
when porches call
but days convene
on autumn's toll

Bryan Scott Bard

Artist's Profile
Richard A. Leddy
Camp Meeker, CA, USA

My father wrote light and humorous verse, and he was known for it. It was by his example that he taught this art to me. When I wrote these silly lines, I had him in mind. But between the time I wrote these lines and the day I received word of this publication, my father died. Death has robbed from me a little joy I wished to share with him. So now, here it is dedicated to him in memorial. To Albert Morray Leddy, may your words never perish so that the world will always have reason to smile.

A Space for Your Thoughts

Can callow coveys
Curry Cupid's favor
With words so clipped they
Have no thoughts to savor?
Is she fair with no
Chosen words to soothe me?
Because of this I
Tarry importunely.
Yet she chirps in shopping mall palaver,
"Oh, my gosh," and "Awesome," with staccato "Cool!"
Where's the time and space for words to mention
A simple thought like
Love? Can words give answer?
Maybe she's the dancer
Who mimes what I perceive from rhymes.
She's the master in the dress-up ballet.
She's the siren, she, barely clad in wool.
So a blushing belly button breaks my stand,
And makes me blindly rush to her fine skill,
As if she stood and gave a loud command.

Richard A. Leddy

Mahogany Justice

You live in a darkened alley
Sleep between the layers of two cardboard boxes
Inside a green tin can used for trash

We exist on both sides of the fence
Yours, I'm told, is tragically wrong
Mine is supposed to be right

We have long talks, but you don't have much to say
I'm too young to understand how
An honest man like you can fall from grace

"An eye for an eye" is what the Good Book says
Innocent until proven guilty sets a criminal free
Just ask my son, my wife, and me

Used to be I could see
The halls of mahogany justice
Working for country, state, and family

Now, thirty years have passed
And I often wonder what happened to you
Can you see
The halls of mahogany justice
Working for country, state, and family?

Gabriel Cavazos

About Death

I miss you.
Technology cannot solve
the distance problem
between you and me—
easier to enter and
photograph our neighboring
galaxy
than to breach the time and space
that separates us.
How strange.
It wasn't long ago
we were hand in hand—
bodies close—solid—physical—
as the gardens we planted or the
firewood we cut with our ancient chainsaw.
Science, that imposter,
cannot bring you back to me.

Jo Ann Knox

At Seven

At seven I play on sticky tar roads, pop
black juicy bubbles with short hairless toes,
and go to bed smelling
of kerosene.
At seven I walk ankle deep into ocean
and stop.
Sunlight shines down into shallow water, refracts and bursts out
in spiked rays.
From hot sand I watch my fearless brother
up to his chest
and wait for clouds.
At seven I sit above
post-monsoon muddy banks,
high in flame trees, hanging fire
flowers over still, chocolate water.
My bare feet, callused and brown,
swing through southeast Asian dusks.

Alexandra Aber Alemi

Limbs

Seeing again the outlines of now-naked trees
outside your bedroom window, I said to you—
"Maybe they're inlines instead,"
meaning maybe the line between limbs and dark sky
is drawn to keep the night out of the tree,
instead of to keep the life in.

After I spoke, you rolled closer in bed, wrapped
your arms around me,
kissed my right shoulder as I watched branches tremble,
tapping lightly, yet hoping you'd hear the faint plea,
rise from the bed, and open the window.

Karyn Lynn Crispo

positive energy can be made to burst

she reads absent fortunes from sweet cookies,
prescribing their remedies to wounded presumptive elements,
and she watches her sickly fish
with inept hands and sadness
scumming the surface, like his water
dotted with tiny bubbles.
she gave him the catchy name, duck,
and he dwelled through the summer.
she placed the fortune:
"one who admires you greatly is
hidden before your eyes by his tank"
along with half a dozen lucky numbers
that just didn't ring of luck.
admiration aside,
fish appear to be crying when they are dying.

Rilee Haiman

Silver Screen

Silent life flickering
Immortal and drained
Liquid memories filtered
Veins slit and shining
Extras peripheral
Ruby-red rewards

Stars in focus, fade to glitter
Conducting diamond double-crossers
Revenge is so retro
Emaciated martyrs
Endlessly dying
Noir lived and died in glamour's wake.

Sharon Boyle

My Father's House

As I stand in my father's house
the smell of years-old tobacco
fills the warm shadows
and hangs on a memory
His skin like the leather
of his empty chair
reminds me of quiet days
behind the sirens of childhood
The curtains that
ripple with a soft hum
blanket me in a gentle lullaby

Jon Boranca

Rocky Times and Sunlight

I trust my life into her.

We . . . are so burdened sometimes.
At times I want to flee,
To find my own path with rain,
Be swallowed by a hole.

But I cannot live without her.
I can't do anything but stick to her,
Cleave to her.
Breathe her in, her glowing skin.

She is mine, me. And I am hers, she.
One. Individual. Two.
Like the faces of temper.
We are the arrangement of earth and moon.

She is living in my tide.

Robert D. Thayne

Artist's Profile
Esr S. Ray
Fayetteville, AR, USA

This poem is about someone who has made mistakes and feels the pain as a result. Sometimes there is no way to change things that have happened, so one stands still, reflects, and tries to appear pleasant to the sight of others. As a person, I take pride in my two most beautiful, loving daughters, sensible sons-in-law, four precious grand daughters, and a thoughtful husband. I live in Fayetteville, Arkansas and work for a highly renowned corporation. ESR is my pen name.

A Pool

Each drop of me is collected in a body
That winds through routines of every day
Melted, talk, walk, bend, bow, get, and give
Steaming and evaporating from top to toes
Then comes the time to gather in me
In a look that's called beautiful
Bare in its core
Battered within, a complete life in its essence
Hidden from sight, but always muddying the surface
With pains for seeking pleasures from when till now
I am a pool of standing-still, fathomless body of mostly water
Bound by its shores, untended, uncared for—
Nature's gift to those who come
To put out the fires of their simmering lives!

Esr S. Ray

Artist's Profile
Santiago Trejo
Brooklyn, NY, USA

I don't remember what was first, the words or my imperfect steps, but in between, I suppose I started to feed my mind with details that, with the coming years, will become beautiful things, then thoughts, then sounds, then poems. Step after step, sidewalks of different cities I left behind, and the world became a commonplace of inspiration. I discovered the power of words and the enchanted web they are able to build, to trap, to enjoy, to fall infatuated, to enamorate, or to live under the energy of magical and powerful language.

After Dinner

Before I had opened the door
it was agreeable; I had recognized your contour.
Already in, I tossed nearest to you
and I lost control of my irises
because you already controlled them,
and they went from your neck to your eyes.

My empties became full;
while my words surrounded your ears,
my lips tried to wake up echoes on yours.
Still I captured something behind your smile,
and my eyes bent to apprehend something at yours.

After I articulated the utters,
I kept for you throughout the day.
I felt how my voice shattered itself in sounds
and traveled to your illuminated ears by stars.

At the end of my everyday-rite dinner,
I found my emotions had been quickened.
I close the door on my way out,
and the huge scenario of the city devours me.

Santiago Trejo

fishbowl of stars

stars: bright fish
in amethyst-dark waters swim
lazily across the fishbowl sky
floating aimlessly across their home of
burning supernovas and swirling wisps
of energy and inviting eternity.
lying on cool dewed wetness,
i want to cup a trickle, a handful
of the shining things: ice-hot, burning cold.
i nod along to the steady rhythm of the universe
quieting and boisterous and i feel small.
so i just listen
to the studded fishbowl waters drift,
a whisper of breeze smelling faintly
of stardust and rose hip. and
between the tails of shooting-star fish
i reach out, anoint myself with ultraviolet
and the fish slowly fade, disappear
one by one.

Spring Lee

Womb

In the mangled hours
Between dusk and dawn
I hear the breathing of the forest as its
Inhabitants weep loudly to the moon
The cries of the coyotes become a
Soundtrack to my dreams and a melody of warning to my nightmares
I am called home
To the sanctuary of night
To the cathedral of earth
To the life that exists far beyond the shelter of my bedroom
Sleep overcomes me
And as my body rests
My soul dances to the lullaby of nature

Emily Dawn Carter

Artist's Profile
Amanda Rivera
Tujunga, CA, USA

My love of poetry began with an enchantment with the music in everyday speech. A poet is not only a storyteller, but a composer of word melodies. In "Waste Away" the song of the rondeau resonates deeply with nostalgia. Like memory, the song of the rondeau is fluid and ephemeral, but returns occasionally with a refrain to remind you of the past. Every day we need to take a moment to digest that precious refrain, however, it might sing to us. That refrain reminds me that what I longed for as a child now feeds my daydreams, and I must make the dreams reality.

Waste Away

A hammock to waste away the day in
with bare feet, gingham skirts, sun-warmed skin.
Wedges of arctic watermelon to go with
the jaw-locking lemonade you bathe in.
Now wipe the summer from your chin.

Along with memory's aching trade in
your braids that little dress is wearing thin.
An office of your own and work to do
with pencils and staples, coffee to brew
to waste away the day in.

Under the roar of voices you swim in
between faxes, calls, promises as thin
as a legal sheet, laughter, music to
make your toes wriggle, and out of the blue
a hammock and dreams that made your head spin,
to waste away the day in.

Amanda Rivera

Artist's Profile
Raymond F. Rogers
Greensboro, NC, USA

"The Muse," not offered for publication before now, was composed as I walked a Greensboro, North Carolina, mail delivery route. Now retired, I am busily planning to have more poems published and available to the public at many bookstores. I have completed a book for my wife of sixty years, "Happy Ever After." "The Muse" she declared a favorite when first written. My delicious wife is Mary Lillian Johnson Rogers.

The Muse

Sometimes when I'm about my work,
Stray words will come to me,
Un-summoned and disorganized,
Like driftwood from the sea.

Sometimes whole phrases brush my mind,
Then teasingly depart,
And oftentimes they seem to rhyme
Their own intrinsic art.

Again, they linger like a kiss,
Arousing quick response,
And I embrace them thinking,
This must be true art this once.

So I will quickly write them down
Before they go away,
In hope that they will find renown
In some far-distant day.

The marriage of those words with thoughts
Would prove to be divine,
Should their brief union find its fruit
In some immortal line.

Raymond F. Rogers

One Misty Monday on the Oregon Coast

Pewter-gray frigates float on mercury-silver
sea. Dull slate storm clouds wall up the sky
with determined drabness. The air smells
like old grease rags and inky, wet
newspapers. A stray beam of sunlight
refuses to reflect off the oil slick
in the parking lot. I sigh.
Even the seagulls look dingy—
well, more than usual.
So I finger a worn 1979 quarter
that smudges my fingertips
and walk an extra block to find
a gum ball machine.
I insert the coin like a widow's mite into
the gray machine's maw, twist the handle—
some steel-aluminum alloy.
I giggle like a four-year-old
when I lift the flap
and find
cheery, cherry red!

Crystie Cook

The Slightest Breeze

She came every summer
slipping in like the slightest breeze,
molding my image and my imagination
and giving compliments that redeemed
an innocent, unloved girl.

Her love made me real
as in the molded wooden puppet boy Pinocchio.
I became what she believed I was—
a real girl,
and someday a woman.

She saw the mean soul of my father
and she told me I would grow beyond it
and she knew this wonderful truth the whole while—and she was right.

She evidenced what real work and real women
were made of,
and I became it under her blanket of
grandmotherly love and care.

Colleen Frances McKee

Done Gone

I'm driving down a stretch of highway just south of Lexington
somewhere between Ohio and Tennessee—
that one that's lined with old, gray antique shops
and rusted-over gas stations and broken down billboards
and Hank Williams is singing on the radio
and I can barely hear him through the static. The song fades away,
then comes back and it reminds me of someone I knew
but I don't want to talk about her right now.
I had to leave town suddenly back there and now I might go to Memphis.
I've never been there but I knew this guy that did and he had fun
so I suppose now is as good a time as any
so I borrowed this car from a friend (though they don't know it yet)
and took off early yesterday
and maybe I'll stop at a rest area and call her and tell her
how I'm going to Memphis and, man,
how I'm gonna paint that town and . . .
no, I can't call her because she'll think I'm thinking about her
and that's a thousand miles from the truth.
She's probably thinking about me right now, regretting what she did.
But I don't want to talk about it.

Josh Michael Compton

From Their Mouths

From the mouths
that name me,
that have witnessed
my death

the thorns
of carbon memoranda
bringing back news of centuries
that will betray me,
as it envisions me,
as it sets up, like blisters,
along
my threaded skin

the words
and their copies, and their
treadmills, and
their riveting silences:
the slow,
dull hum
of a nineteenth-century worker—

you're next on my list, my list that won't end

Cameron Martin Reid

Cruel

This is a new sort of pain,
it is the sort that dances around me.
It encircles me and taunts me.
It goes through and through me,
soaking into me, leaving me like a sponge.
I am wrung out, hung out to dry.
Alone and lonely in the cruel, rough
unforgiving wind.

Lisa S. Pennell

Breath

I walked back down there,
To the murky waters
Where we had once been,
And I lost my breath,
And I looked through the forest
For anything that would burn.
All I could find were memories,
And then a fondness in life hit me:
Words . . .
All I could hear were your words.
They seemed to whisper in the gusts,
And as the gusts blew the coals against my skin,
It felt like you were touching me
And I lost my breath.
As I backtracked through my mind,
You were touching me
With inspiration,
Your words, your wisdom,
And the peace of mind you put me in.
You were my breath.

Jesse H. Cole

Beer in Bryant Park
For GH

Because I love you
each moment we spend together is never
enough . . .
Reaching across time and distance
imagining your laughter
night after night . . .
because I love you
reality speaks too softly and
you are my lost hope—an
answer that has
no question.
Together we breathe life into the
past . . .
afraid of forgetting the
reasons we do this while
keeping new souvenirs of today.

Norma Joan Meade

String Quartets

Funerals and reunions have a blurred
border in my family.
The reunion after Tim's
funeral brought us all together again,
everyone eating dry sandwiches,
and me staring, fascinated by the end
of my shoe.
Penderecki wrote
string quartets that remind me of that day;

all buzzing and noise and who knows
what to say?
Then, a hand on my shoulder
and my father's voice is a cello,
a recognizable melody. I don't remember
his words, though the timbre stays
with me.
Sometimes at night
I mistake two passing trains for music.

Beth Chapman Broyles

Artist's Profile
W. Christopher Epler
Albuquerque, NM, USA

I have no idea where this poem came from, but it's friendly enough. Perhaps poetry is my escape hatch from mathematics (I'm a mathematician). I guess sometimes you just need to smell the pencils. And may I thank all those poetry folk over the years who keep sharing with me things you can only see out of the corners of your eye.

a little something

a yellow wooden pencil,
tubelike,
and pointed at one end,
rubbery and red at the other,
is surprisingly hexagonal.
the black lead peeks out uncertainly,
waiting to serve some purpose
unknown to its imprisoned eraser head.

the marriage between the eraser
and the pipe of lead
within the truck of wood
is discretely hidden by a thin metal crown.
this pencil has already lost its virginity,
leaving thin marks
intelligible to something somewhere.

it's larger than an ant,
and smaller than an elephant,
but so are a great many things.

W. Christopher Epler

Artist's Profile
Kristen Booth
New York, NY, USA

The subject of this poem was quite simple to choose. I love my city and recently have had to endure too many put-downs and insults about her from those I'd rightly call my friends. I'll respect their opinion when they even feign effort to visit for the first time in their small residence.

Love Letter to the City, 2002

Within a blink, sapphire tubes of neon
And Kodachrome reflect back at you
From within a tiny cirque of a soul.
Breath. Beat. Light.
A reckless curl impedes the view.
Nic, nic, nictitate—too impatient
To wait.
The lady
She keeps calling me, no matter what.
The nay-sayers nay-say.
I've got my kind of love here
Waiting for me downtown.
Six train from Astor Place. Spiny stiletto heels.
Jet-black jacket and glass-keen lips
That rival Chrysler's gleam and the call of the Crystal Lounge.

New York City.
I'll never let you down, known all over town.
Have known it all along;
In your arms is where I belong.

Kristen Booth

Artist's Profile
Larry Coe Prater
Wichita, KS, USA

I have exchanged letters with James Dickey from 1972 until his death in 1997. How sad poems published in America/Kansas Quarterly/Arkansas Review/ Arkansas River Review have a poem. "Blues for F. Scott" in the Fitzgerald Authors, USA, Columbia, South Carolina.

The Visit

Broken light has come down through the trees
And rests on my father's grave, here
In the small, Missouri cemetery I return to
When I most want to die.

All of the light of evening is here;
Each tree's leaf holds it a moment
Before it falls to the winter's dead grass.

A ghost of a moon has begun turning the trees
The color of water.
My breath is around my head
Like a helmet, and I remember the first I wore,
That my father brought home from Normandy

To me as a small child,
And the winter before he died,
When, in a Blue-Norther, I saw him make
The longest, purest wing-shot I ever saw in my life.

Now geese are flying above;
They sound near the stars.

Larry Coe Prater

Earthtouch

I walked in empty fields,
furrowed rows of rich soil beneath
my feet softly.
How like my life,
this windswept solitude
before we met.
A bird cries out—
sad, sweet song of existence—
to an empty world. No echo,
no answering cry from lead-gray sky
or the silent earth.

My heart is like the bird.
You are my song and my echo.

Elizabeth Bogue

The Lighthouse

A lighthouse stands on the brow of a hill,
Red tile roof pressing hot against the sun.
Her beacon beamed afar the caution shrill,
Sound passage can often be a rocky one.

Nearby gun emplacements look mutely on,
Sentinel against an enemy long gone.
Her memory escapes that time astutely,
Forgotten now the drill to quick respond.

Reed tight against the wind she stands,
Evoking memories of a time long past.
Fancies in a dim recall military bands,
And white billows blowing from a mast.

Abaft a picket fence a sleeping garden lies,
Bulwarked against a savage, wolfish wind.
She sighs in light of memory, then espies
A coast made safe by sea dogs who defend.

Nikki Campbell

Artist's Profile
Joan Gettry
Beechhurst, NY, USA

When I wrote this poem in 1995, it came at a time when my thoughts were rampant and prolific, and although many of my poems were published by the International Library of Poetry, rummaging through my manuscript, after receiving this invitation, I thought this poem very appropriate because it spoke to me and of me. This I had not recognized before.

What Is Rigidity?

It's nothing more than a stranglehold that
Grasps the mind and body into a vise.
It gives no flexibility for bending or moving
Nor does it loosen the vise of contraption.

What a world! What a loss
This monster of rigidity surrounds itself in!
It sees nothing, except what it wants to see.
It hears nothing, except for the sounds
Of its own recordings.

It swims into its own ripples of a stream
And above all, it misses the delicate aroma
Of various fragrances of life and opportunity
And imbues its own odor of stunted growth, and
A lackluster of a sense of belonging, and thus,
Misses the momentum of thrust forward and upward.
This is the world of rigidity;
This is the world rigidity encompasses.

Joan Gettry

Genetics

Experts say that genes skip
a generation.
You laugh like your grandmother.
You love like your aunt.

But biology's spiders wrap long-
neglected chandeliers,
and the curse of memory invades
unguarded moments,

distorting prisms that once sparkled
reds and yellows, now wrapped taut
like unopened presents
from strangers.

Ann Dorsett Ecoff

"Semper Fidelis"

And in the midnight hours of my heart
When sun gives way to moon and crystal stars
When roses turn away and dim lights find
A way to live beneath my eyes and hide
I hold you to my soul and in I breathe
Your mystery and love's complexities
With not a word to stumble from my lips
We watch a world's eternity that lived
In shadows, as we lay in candlelight
Yet holding fast to this, our only night
As I will be a dream by next sunrise
Without you I live not a worthy life
Until, at last, your lips may find my own
I'd live to die most faithful, yet alone

Lauren Elisabeth Wilmoth

juniper

there were no kisses
when the juniper grew
but when the juniper died
weren't we always kissing

and lying with our hair back
on the sand like nettles
green in the morning?

Kristen Walker

I Dreamt Again

I dreamt I was an oasis in barren soil,
barren land. A healing spring. A fountain
of my grandmother's youth, I was a siren
to be used by God. A marigold in shades
of red, I was a river by a sea of flowerbeds.
I was a mountain, short and defiant,
strong as I was proud. Hallowed I, sacred,
hallowed ground. That I am. That thing I
tried to be. Mountain that I was. But now,
what's become of me? I dreamt I was a
river fighting against a bigger sea.
Swallowed up, engulfed by the current. That
was free. Moved I was by the greater
force. Imagine this of me. Thrashed
against the rocks of foaming water washed
against the sand. Bathing seashells
in my blood. Nourishing again. Once
barren soil, barren sand. Leaving the sea
salty with my tears.

Marie Deniese Hoggs

Not by Might

Like the leaves of the forest when summer is green,
That legion with their banners at sunset was seen;

Like the leaves of the forest when autumn has blown,
That legion on the desert lay withered and strewn.

For the angel of Death spread his wings on the blast,
And breathed in the face of the enemy as he passed.

And the eyes of the daunted waxed deadly and chill,
And their hearts that once panted forever grew still!

And the widows of the Great City are loud in their wail,
And the idols are broke in the City of Hell.

And the might of the "Evil Ones" unscathed by the sword,
Has melted like snow in the gaze of the Lord!

Cindy T. Lea

The Night a Part of Us

When an owl flies across the Jack pine,
The knowing beat of its wings
Reassures the soft us
That darkness is also quiet and safe
And that some creatures and some thoughts
Move only in darkness.
An owl is only hunting mice, after all,
And thoughts are just words.
As mortals we need the wings beating
To make the night complete.
We need to see more than a hunter
To make the darkness apart of us.
We need the words
To make the night a part of us.

Cynthia Elizabeth Haiste

Artist's Profile
Susan Lynn Oberg
Philadelphia, PA, USA

There is a stealthy monster inside some of us called panic disorder. One who suffers from PD undergoes the effects of a short-circuited fight or flight response sent from the brain. This response goes off whenever it wants, whether you're delivering a speech or lying in bed. I wrote "schedule four" at a time when I dreaded facing another day. It only meant more suffering. "schedule four" is a bit of a rough read, but I needed to share this with the literary community, with the world. We all have our ways of exorcising demons and of battling monsters.

schedule four
Dedicated to the sufferers

mick sang about mother's little helper
daughter's got one too
she goes running for the shelter
five pills in the morning
two or three at night
i'm stabilized for a little while
i'm feeling better for a short time
then the pain
oh god the pain
it grows stronger every day
i wake up with it
it sleeps under my tear-stained pillow
i don't know how much longer i can hold on
not give in to the pain
how much longer i can survive
this body is crumbling down around me
and i am trapped inside
how much longer
oh god the pain

Susan Lynn Oberg

Artist's Profile
Patricia Maureen Saddlemire
Glastonbury, CT, USA

I use poetry to reflect a moment in time that could not otherwise be captured. "Womanly Reflections" was written for my daughter, Christina, then age twelve. As she stood before a mirror, I was reminded of an instant a generation earlier when my mother saw me in a similar moment in distress, thus somehow creating a timeless connection between all mothers and daughters.

Womanly Reflections

I laughed
when I saw you standing there,
stark naked,
in front of a full-length mirror,
wondering when your womanly attributes
would appear.

Your frown told me
you could not see
reflected there,
another straight-lined girl
from another time
whose mother once caught a glimpse
of her concern etched upon a mirror.

What a beauty you will be!
If only I could tell you that
to ease your present pain.
But time will be your teacher
and, perhaps, one day
the gentle words of a lover
will redefine your reflection.

Patricia Maureen Saddlemire

Forbidden Art

Scratched frames
heavy with dusty plastic,
contrast
black borders
mixed with faded paint,
reflect
hidden emotion
scarred with ancient time,
shatter
dull thoughts
lined with dark boredom,
bring
true imagination
created with proud hands,
awaiting
silent admiration
soaked in life's tears
forever.

Sara Renaud

soliloquy

you have gone
and life unfolds without you
waking does not bring your face
nor all those early-morning sounds
the inner ear is tuned to
memories play havoc
with the heavy-hanging hours
mirages tease the senses
in this endless desert of your absence
where suddenly the timbre of a voice
or similarity of stride
quickens the pulse with expectation
for some stubborn hidden core
still clings to disbelief
then as you walk away
on stranger's legs
across the concrete dunes
another stone of anguish
drops with hollow sound
into the vacuum you have left behind.

Esther Kunda

after love

summer falls once more
november days subsist to my surprise
navi shines no brighter and capella
does not dim at all
for even the moons persist in their rotation
every planet holds its place so i
collect the thought of us
garner hints of our love and
capture our endless melody of laughter
i stretch each one into the distance

amidst the way we smelled were the
late saturday mornings in bed and
our quiet breathing alongside it
was us fattening each other's minds with
fresh schemes and dewy abstractions

the remembrance of our love is scantly
more than the tingling, pulsing, that
demanding scent or us
i am missing
the theory of you

Myra Lynn Maybin

Plowed Fields

In the middle
of his fresh-plowed field,
the farmer kneels,
scooping up the good earth
with cupped hands
to feel it
(as a parent would check
the forehead of a child
for a fever or chill)
and to smell its subtle
fragrance of humble temples
and earthworm empires.

Overhead, a red-tailed hawk
rides the wind,
working faint furrows into
its own blue prairie field.

Linda L. Schneider

The Wind

Listen to the wind
A voice within a voice
A language known by an untaught ear
Listen to the wind
Breath recognizing breath
Creation mirrors itself in you
The wind plays tag
Churning nervous atoms into pliable clay
The form in human and breathes
Catch the wind in open hands
Loose a kiss upon the breeze
Grasping fingers net a too-familiar flesh
Ever been kissed by a shadow
Ever been embraced by a God
The wind blows wherever it wills
Full faltering years find you in a dark place
You fall into something that loves
The night reveals the treasures of darkness
Yield to the all-encompassing wind
The wind gives you God.

John Lee

Three Women and Not a Hero

Hey there, my darling dangereuse,
Come with me and see a vision
Of Amy in the morning with pears.
Let us sing ludicrously and find ourselves suddenly alone.
For Geraldine will sing with eyes to the moon
And trees in your mind will try
To grow and grab you.
But once I thought I'd write a song
About heroes or earrings, then my cx called
And cried on the phone.
And once the soft sound of an "aah"
Collided with the "unh unh unh"
Of heroic rock and roll, and I thought,
It might be pleasant to die for something,
Like the way your lips turn up
When you're about to lie.
Come listen to my beautiful,
My darling dangereuse,
My song has made you a hero.

Kathryn Grace Philbrook

Untitled

I wove flowers into my hair in the evening,
like small pieces of porcelain digging
into my flesh, protruding
softly so that you could hear them
like chips of ice every time
my feet hit the floor.
But you looked out the many windows
and dreamed of other worlds.
So I wove flowers into my hair in the afternoon
like glowing coals that breathed softly
on the back of my neck
and flared to life when you drew near,
but you never realized that,
even as one hand reached out to touch them,
your entire body recoiled.
So I wove flowers into my hair in the early morning,
ashes that called to you, but you crawled
toward your carved runes of self-preservation
and bottled up your soul;
you watched and dreamed, but never knew.

Cheresse Estelle Burke

April

The memories of that other place
appear sometimes.
Like a watery heart
in the bottom of a plastic bottle.

I would walk through fog
past the god reduced to grey stone bricks
avoiding the cracks and the space
under the sky.

You were the yellow.

And I told you again and again
but the words rubbed off on my hand
smudging.

Leaving a streak like a tear.

Hana Sullivan

Artist's Profile
Diana Jaleh Arya
Seattle, WA, USA

This poem reflects my relationship with my brother. My father would love taking our picture together, and many times we would be forcing a smile after a fight over toys, the remote control, etc. I'm a teacher in Seattle, Washington.

Wrestling Alligators

A picture of us squished in a lawn chair
With painted smiles and plastic shoes
Choosing to give into the stiff posture of brother and sister,
Hands held tightly in strangulation, nerves twisted in stagnate air.
Chairs scream across the sky as colors
Fade into something less familiar.
A distance numbs the countless battles that never found victory.
Regret rises from the debris and consumes
The vacancy between us.
One last pose—an "alligator crossing" sign.
We cling to our last effort of portraying inseparable siblings,
Hands reach to remember
The fishhook scars and punched-arm bruises.
We grow a smile of our own and wait for the flash.

Diana Jaleh Arya

Two Sticks

Two sticks he held the early man
embraced and forced by frenzied hands
that friction implement his plan
Warmth pronounced to glow and grew
the way enlightened, he passes through
Does not the finger enhance the hand
and at arm's length thus extend the man
Do we not reach to grasp or clutch
at things beyond our sense of touch
Two sticks he held the early man
in place on mobile launching pad
Warmth pronounced to glow and grew
the way enlightened he passes through

Paul Adrain Hodgkin

Summer Afternoon, New York City

As the sun with its fiery tongue
licked skyscrapers clean and
struck like stone against the flinty streets,
we lay in labellate splendor, each to each
in our quiet cove, our cool
retreat. Between lambent
leaves of golden light,
we shimmered like labradorite.
While weary workers toed their marks
and car horns blared and fenders sparked
and vendors hawked and sirens whirled,
my hand in yours, our fingers
curled. A pas de trois, adagissimo,
the two of us and the waning glow.

Terri Kirby Erickson

Artist's Profile
Michelle Leigh Rodgers
North Little Rock, AR, USA

As a physician, I have been given the unique opportunity to experience the heights and depths of the human condition. It is through writing that I attempt to understand myself and those around me. I also realize that experience makes us different but living makes us the same.

Mercury

A heavy heart
pushing blood like mercury throughout this
body,
such a low boiling point—
rising, falling in regards to my ambient
temperament
Temperature?
Beautiful, but toxic
Spilled, but not
Just rolling away from you despite, to spite,
your efforts to contain me
Can you read me?
Shake me down into cooler
numbers?
Use me as a guide or disregard me as a fluke?
Pin me down with your tongue, and I will
surely boil, rise
Bite me, and I will
make you mad as a hatter
Trapped in glass with only dreams of
freedom, of havoc, I live a quiet, useful life

Michelle Leigh Rodgers

Prairie Torn

Raised between lakeshore and farmland, the harsh grandeur
Of Superior, the golden sweep of prairies,
He measured the elements and found his balance.
Summers on the farm, racing the wind through the fields,
Free of the cold house on the bluff overlooking
The lake and city. Music made the silent halls
Sing. He painted stark walls with imagination
And found solitary solace by the shore. Then,
Grandfather dead, the farm gone, and only the lake
To ease the lonely burden of expectations.
The only son, the golden one, trapped by family
Dreams. The scales weighted to money, power, success.
No time to chase moonbeams, no room for second best.
He measured the elements and lost his balance.

Meredith Anne Elliott

Seeing Dark

And what is this to me
That causes time to circle back
To sit cat-like and dark,
An old familiar,
Long rid of,
Purged, so to speak, by letting go.
And now this low moan
Gurgling to the night
Like the gibbous moon
Beyond a cloud . . . still,
And in the palest cut of silver
A promise barely failed for lack of turning.

Ira W. Claxton

Artist's Profile
Priscilla Stone
McNeal, AZ, USA

Poetry is a gift from God. I thank the Lord Jesus Christ for endowing me with such. I wrote this poem regarding the only mortal man who has ever truly loved me. The Welshman will always inspire deep passion in my soul. Thank you.

There Is a Fire in the Welshman

His mind is quick and playful
His heart is deep and pure
Inside this rugged package
Is intensity and sweet demure
Beneath his chiseled features
Below his blood and bone
There is a fire in the Welshman
That very few have known
I've seen it in the morning
I've felt it in the eve
It has smoldered every breath of mine
Unto its flame I cleave
I've tasted ash upon his lips
And smelled the smoke progress
I've heard it roar through fields of me
And laid down my soul for less
Along the heated pathways
Beneath the flaming trees
There is a fire in the Welshman
That consumes an icy tease

Priscilla Stone

Timeline

The day we drank cider
Blessed the double moon
Rolling on a
Disused railway station
Later
Hid on the old abbey roof
Picked up drunken Jack
From under his car

The day we got up
Five o'clock in the morning
Walked round the village
As silent as stars

This English child
So sure of the future
Wide-eyed and feckless
Push your bike
Like pushing your own soul
Out of the screaming blue sky

Philip Nigel Unwin

Cigarettes at Midnight

There is not enough light here, yes? No?
We're singed into our corners,
blackened edges and yellowed skin,
straining to read this smudged ink and my
Braille cigarette burns, hot under your
twitching fingers.
They say much more than I ever could.
Lower than my paper-crisp guts
there is no weight this side of the compass;
it tingles, it breathes,
whispers words like "membrane"
and slips upstairs for the exhalation
when it all becomes much less than love.
As basic, as moody as bricks and cement,
four building piles of terra-cotta effacement
boxed coyly, lidded by a sky black and clear
as a spider's five thousand jewel eyes
and the stars, all the stars: a flickering,
florescent light squeezing through the
pinpricks in my ink-stained blotterboard.

Declan Nyall Greene

Jessica

I am forgetting the forever motions—
my hair gets longer and I grow over you,
the phone forgets your name; we have lake
swimming memories, incredible comic strips
written in silly high school hand and sunny
days skipping school, laughing drives
through Florida rain, singing loud at scary
turns—dressing up and dressing down
pretentious poetry and devastating diary
one in a million on a race to the moon
vision freed of what will not be between a
long and short-haired girl: No neon
neighbors, sweet sugar-sharing Shiloh
your laughter dwindles down the road.
I'm standing at the shallow of a valley in
a ghost town of our grievances, and the
sight of a swelling dam in seven years
predicts an abundance of love but I cannot
guarantee that I'll remember
what I'm forgetting now.

Cassie L. McDaniel

Summer Night

Silence of the night
dark blue velvet
soft and deep.

In my ears sounds of summer
pulsing faint echoes . . .
crickets ticking in some far-off field.

The moon is late tonight
its cold light cools the warm land
as I fall asleep.

Lorna Bowlby West

Artist's Profile
Nathan Stewart
East Liverpool, OH, USA

In a sometimes mundane world, poetry is the voice which haunts me and brings me to my knees to cry out in that sullen tone. Then, at the deepest moment, poetry becomes the light of God showering hope and warmth over our spirits.

Liberty

It was innocence that bled there,
unsure, unaware, and not withstanding.
The lady watched her quelled city tremble,
her people's red become fire,
blood become ashes, stone become flesh.

None would come to doubt,
those who felt the pangs and took the bruises,
that her salient hand still held the torch
high above the wounded world.

And in the rubble burns an epitaph
faint and furious in her name;
believe it when someone dies for you,
takes a place in a burning building for you,
receives a bullet so that you may live.

There is no greater monument than she.

Nathan Stewart

Tanka for Two: Relationship

My father rides on
A bicycle built for two
Past Mother's garden.

He tips his hat towards her.
An empty seat follows him.

She is elbow deep
In mud and does not look up.
She is hoping for

Some green life to grow. She digs
Deeper and deeper. Nothing.

Kirsten Olson

While Reading

Sweltering nights. Silence. Homer.
The book is laying half-opened.
Odysseus is still longing
For the great return to his Ithaca.

Inconceivable
That all you great Greek men
Left your homes
For one flirty redhead.

The same wind is turning my pages
That once filled your sails.

But the midnight is almost here
And I will shake off my worries
Like sand in my sneakers
When leaving the beach behind.

Elizabeth Pyjov

Artist's Profile
Edward V. Johnson
Old Hickory, TN, USA

Growing up on a farm in central Illinois, I developed a concern for farmers whose livelihood depends upon the weather. An article on the dust bowl tragedy of the 1930s inspired this poem, which I dedicate to farmers everywhere in appreciation of their hard work, their perseverance, and their courage.

Rain-Song Drummer

In early summer,
I listened for the Rain-Song Drummer
To ease the thirsty, drying plain,
To keep it thriving green and strong.
But no rain and no song.

Late that summer,
I longed to hear the Rain-Song Drummer.
I heard the dying land complain;
The days were hot and much too long
With no rain and no song.

In early fall,
I heard the hungry cattle bawl,
And dust storms swept the grassless plain,
A once-rich land no longer strong.
Still no rain and no song.

Late that fall,
The Rain-Song Drummer made his call,
But not a farmer could remain.
The Drummer stayed away too long
With his rain and his song.

Edward V. Johnson

Chimera

The state line yawns,
expanding her pregnant belly
to push us out and away
from this swell of alluvion.
I cannot live
with him or without him.
My heart is cracked concrete.
His thunderous words bittersweet—
unthinkable.
Swarming over me for killer sting.
Colloquial excruciation
our clandestine marriage of soul
our fruitless vine
untwists
into smoky exaltation,
the grave of separation
suspended flaming fog
in the citronella-scented breeze.

Chantal Forrest

On Series

I had the Fibonacci series
tattooed on my back
but the nautilus remains empty

truth and beauty in the universe
and order ordered according to
order

found brother right in a two-dollar ruler
and in hyperbola
what she represented

to the man in the gutter
lying tangent to the curb
maximizing the principle

Cheryl Anne Ricks

"De Profundus Clamo Altac Dominae"

On the surface of this lake

rings from fish rising at dusk
distort and crown the reflected peaks
from the range of South Sierras

behind, imbued now with a sense
of glory or grace and cloaked

in sacramental white. Each fish

seems to ignorantly cast spells of faith
with every catch of insect: An act

of survival or sacrifice. Then, the trout
descends to the belly of the lake where
it might fin through decay of centuries
of once life matter that turns through drafts
of water from the end of its tail, always
to settle in the soul of haloed Sierras.

David M. Morgan

My Love for You

Seven herons, slate, shin-deep,
stockstill, staring into what's swirled
by them on the ebb. This is how

I knew I would never leave you:
The stab, blink, the stilletoed-head tipped
backwards, the quick, coiled neck stretched
skyward to swallow.

Mathew James Mannion

Untitled

Arm curled under me,
I fell asleep.
I dreamt of twisting
And contortions and
Bent things, like
Rivers and veins and
You.
I woke up, surfacing
From the depths of
A boundless ocean.
The light of the rising sun
Caught on millions of water-facets.
The beauty of fragmented day
Overcame me.
But when I tried to swim,
I found that my
Twisted arm had atrophied,
And now I can only tread water
And wait to regain my strength.

Chris Daniel Shirley

Queen Bee

Why this rain at my windowsill?
Has the queen passed?
And these tears, God's will?

Dropping a new beginning
Reflecting a vivid memory

Like the first time I heard the Blue Hornet Band play
The howl of night stained with electricity
That red-hot sound cutting through the air of the café
I was tripping lights fantastic as I shook and swung
But that was then
Now the beat at my window is playing rhythm
And those songs go unsung

I guess the blues will always be blue
And the bee meant to sting
Somewhere up above us is an angel
And I can still hear her sing

Timothy Jerome Vorhies

Artist's Profile
Nina Camille Dennis
Lansdale, PA, USA

When I write, a flood of thoughts and emotions pours from my mind and forms poetry. This poem describes events within the last year that have changed my life and helped me mature. I am a nineteen-year-old junior at Howard University. My favorite poet is my grandmother, Andrea Edmonds, and I hope to reach her level of insight one day. I would also like to thank my parents, Michele and Brian Dennis, for giving me all that I have ever needed and for allowing me to journey down my own paths.

Reborn

It was jazz from New York City,
smooth and rough, that
tousled my hair
fierce as pain could be.
It was crisp, and it gave birth to me.
It was harmony of time,
a cool, modest placement of you and I,
chance of numbers,
chance of space.
It was ancient,
always standing in place.
I caught up to destiny, and it embraced me.
It was silk from childhood past,
learned of the world,
roaming the land,
cursing and dancing,
soaring with glee.
It was fire, and it became me.

Nina Camille Dennis

untitled

somehow,
the nights seem darker here—smokey and physical—
a southern gentleman.
there is a certain street
i drive down often—
trees bowed above broken asphalt—
and something primal awakens in me,
sense memories tasting of the past,
and i am pulled further in.
how odd that i should land here,
learn to stand here, and all the while
hearing the whisper of
that sweetly familiar "been here before."
sometimes, i wonder what it would be like
to peek inside god and see his plan,
neatly framed, symmetrical, and sane,
labeled with my name—then—
the sighs of the sleepy south call me back,
cradling me safe at last. . . .

Jayne Meyers

The Dogs Watch

Three dogs watch very small children
shooting rockets into the 9 a.m. sun.
A stream of hot sparks rains down on the
compressed stones and dirt of the road.

The dogs stare, half-playful, feet splayed,
ready to chase, half a snarl and their
hackles just lifted. They stand ready,
expectant. One is black.

The children's hard feet are a solid
connection with the earth. The current
flows up through their feet and legs
and bursts from their fingertips in blasts

of golden light like confetti. Wax matches
serenely handled by miniature fingers.
The long hair of the one girl swinging
fine and close to the lighting fuses.

Preschool pyrotechnics. The dogs
watch carefully. Tongues slack,
lolling over teeth. Eyes following
every busy hand like food or fear.

R. Gabrielle Shaw

Artist's Profile
Sherry Keown
Warren, MI, USA

"Perhaps . . . a Song" was written for JBJ, much like a poet himself.
He shakes his head in wonder as tears fog his eyes, as they do mine.

Perhaps . . . a Song

He absently brushes the hair from his eyes,
his attention focused on the stark,
blank page before him. The pen moves across his fingers,
and he leans back and waits for the words
and images to start their dizzying spin.

He writes about love and life, undying friendship,
as well as his broken heart. He closes his eyes,
seeing only a white page, believing that fate
would step in and do its part.

His pen moves silently across the page.
His dreams take flight as a story suddenly unfolds,
visual and stunning, coming from his heart,
as emotion quietly slips into the folds.

He smiles contently; you see what he sees
as his fair hair once again cascades into his eyes.
He knows that through his words you become part of his dream.
Through his words, you could never be blind.
Is it a poem he created, or perhaps a song
he found lounging listlessly,
in the dark recesses of his mind. . . .

Sherry Keown

a celebration

last night
the drought broke
the earth renewed with the promise
of rains
as you smiled
breaking forth a fresh
deluge of hope
in this dried soul

and like the earth
welcoming the rains
arms outstretched
i greeted you
wrapped you
in
gentle embraces
drank
of
the ever-verdant hope
. . . as the rains came . . .

Noelle Jacqueline Ingledew

Ol' Groan

Sundered soft romances can hurt the heart
like a thump,
and crash the crystal labyrinths of your very soul
with one clink.
So ever after soft pale moons stain the sky like dried flakes of skin
the cells now ossified and emptied of the life once there.
Starch plain factory bread where once was crust and crumb
of pungent loaves loved by gentle hands of caring cooks.
Straight asphalt flattened black beneath your feet,
over the crooked water run paths of ragweed or daffodil.
Even plastic orchids weep for their former soul,
and ivy creeps against the grain of Man.
But suns under a lover's darkened brow
are terrible
in the most mundane way
in that soft afternoon light sickens you with its oh-so-usual trill
and neons lights don't drive you crazy anymore.
But then I guess you're ready to live in the world built sans rhyme
and board the train of our dread tempered time.

John-Edgar Martin Lopez

Artist's Profile
Margaret Elizabeth Cone
Tulsa, OK, USA

My poetry often takes root during times of hardship in my life. As this is one of my earlier works, it expresses my angst at feeling the loss of my childish flights of fancy and being grounded by logic. I shall continue to grow and I hope others can find a place in the expression of my own discoveries.

Consequence

One consequence,
Our feathers slowly plucked
Until the air-filled foundation
Of our wings is shackled to dust.

Why is winter viewed as barren
When her womb swells thick with blood,
The bodies of slender saplings
Encased in powdered love?

For all we know, all is perfect,
Just letters connected to thoughts.
Our consequence is in our query,
Yet to stay earthbound is to rot.

Margaret Elizabeth Cone

Artist's Profile
Holly J. Helscher
Wyoming, OH, USA

Clarissa Pinkola Estes speaks of women who are "angel mothers." Julia is one of those individuals. Her consistent, gentle guidance and nurturing helped me turn a corner in my life at a time when I was confused and despairing. Since I have known her, she has helped me put a feminine face on the divine, and as a result, has helped me to see the feminine divine in myself. This poem is a tribute to her as a person and to the grace and wisdom she has bestowed upon me. The world is enriched because of her presence in it.

Julia

To she who has become my mother

You told me once that no one is more earthy than you.
Over time, I have come to understand what that means.

You wear yourself like a black panther,
elegant and graceful,
at home in the spaces you have chosen.

You speak your words like the evergreens,
poised and universal,
unwavering where they stand.

You share your spirit like the glistening moon,
gentle and consistent,
radiating light into shadow.

Connected to all that is,
your earthiness is like a spring meadow,
vibrant and welcoming to those who care to notice.

Holly J. Helscher

Y d J

You should have fled when you could
the short summer of '89—a wild mare
that wouldn't be harnessed
Time's fated grasp nearly caged her flight
but
you would've been safe on her back
far above
out of reach
from the dark arms of even the tallest city towers
and cold prisons where lonely people
slowly choke on the same dreams
where late-night streets sprayed with water
become dark, wet rivers
wherein reflections of tired electric eyes
sleepily glitter
and desperate ones like you
dragged down
under
the burden of heavy iron hearts
drown

Wessel Wessels

Poetry

My cousin's full fat figure
Lies flat against the stairway
Where she is sprawled.
The multicoloured beads scattered,
Framing her fall,
The perfect crime scene.

But this victim, though not dead, weeps
While her mother scolds from the bottom, looking up,
About socks and running and dangers
To two-year-old boys,
And I think, gazing down, like a god from the heavens
Seeing all, yet strangely removed,
This is poetry.

Katherine Chen

Artist's Profile
William Allen Holt
Fort Worth, TX, USA

"Unfinished" is a deliberately understated poem of appreciation for my wife of thirty-seven years, a distinguished educator of young children, now retired, who still works as a volunteer in elementary school. She taught kindergarten, first grade, and special education classes before becoming an assistant principal and then a principal of a large K-4 campus, after which she retired. A colleague once said of her, "She could teach a rock to read." I teach college English myself, a much easier job than my wife, and occasionally publish books, poems, and short articles.

Unfinished

Some things she leaves unfinished—
coffee, pasta, cherry pie, harsh words,
projects that can complete themselves—
all things temporal, binding, growing—
gifts to a world that must after all feed
on leftovers, beg for mercy, finish
its never-ending business.
Finishing only what she must,
this woman, knowing herself unfinished,
gauges her time,
its width and its length,
tastes her moment, tills little fields
that others may harvest
while she moves on.
She cheats time by filling it full,
taking only what she requires
to complete herself in time as,
incompletely and gladly,
I watch her and I learn.

William Allen Holt

Artist's Profile
Christopher Lee Berie
Cranberry Township, PA, USA

This poem was inspired by the idea that humans grieve for loss in so many different ways. In the poem, the guests, who are there to remember the dead and to support this poor woman, can't understand why she isn't mourning as they feel she should be. The beauty of grief, however is that it never fits any particular mold. The overwhelming process of letting go can often bring with it a feeling of guilt, and while this is hard enough, feeling that she never loved him fully in life is what ultimately causes her sadness over his death.

A Procession

She watched them approach with roses,
One in particular with a child clinging to her leg,
Four fingers precariously protruding from pink, red lips.
White knuckles, muttered prayers, whiter eyes
Searching, seeking, scrutinizing this home,
The way the light fell on the thick air,
The way she didn't look scared, angry, lost.
Their own faces—blank canvases for emotional artistry.
Like pilgrims, they brought food and prayer.
And she thought, as they consoled her,
Of her kitchen on this winter morning—
Icicles dripping beyond the glass,
Footfalls of coffee into an empty cup,
How sunlight stained the linoleum before.
As their hands rubbed her black muslin
And condolences extended were received,
Her tears were not for her boy in the earth,
But that she hadn't really loved him.

Christopher Lee Berie

Artist's Profile
Elizabeth Marie Ormsbee
Newark, NY, USA

I am an alumni of Keuka College and now a student at SUNY Brockport, studying English and education. Most of my poems, including those published here, celebrate the lessons I have learned from life, love, and the wonderful strength I see in my closest family and friends. I give many thanks to all who have been there when I stumbled on life's path, and whose inspiration helped me to find my footing again.

Someday

Someday this ring won't
Cut its tell tale mark into my skin.
Someday that haunting melody
Won't tease the tears to fall.
Someday my youth will fade,
Convenience, perhaps,
Content in another face.
Someday I may forgive myself
For everything you have replaced.

Elizabeth Marie Ormsbee

Thunder

Tonight we had thunder but no rain
A boisterous announcement
With no follow-through
And we're left longing for relief
From the oppressive heat and stale air

The evening's blackness is no more revealing
A glimmer of lightning teases our delirium
With phantoms of reality

We sit in this close, stale room
Waiting anxiously for the promise of thunder
The blinding flash of insight, the cloudburst
But they never come

A cold beer holds more promise
Moisture trickles down the bottle
While the amber liquid cools and numbs
From the inside out, our only hope

A faint breeze stirs our drunken stupor
Telling us the storm has passed us by
Again

Charlene A. Derby

Every Superhero Has One Weakness

I'd wear a cape all the time
if society deemed it acceptable.
Every time I'd leave I'd scream,
"Up, up and away!"
Old ladies would ask me to
carry them across the street,
to get their cats out of trees,
to marry their daughters.
To fly, cape dancing in the
teary-eyed wind, tubes from
my nose falling to the ground.
Cancer can't beat a superhero,
that's for sure.
I laugh at it, and cough a little.
To cape, perchance to dream.

Eric Christian Olsen

Artist's Profile
Michael Andrew Kingcaid
Allentown, PA, USA

In a twisted way this poem symbolizes the opinion that you need to be true to youself and not fall victim to peer pressure or even society's guidelines of what is acceptable. It was scribbled down in about ten minutes in a notebook during a boring class in college in October of 1987. It remains unrevised except for some punctuation fixes. I write lyrics as well as poems and I hope to soon have an entire book of my poetry published. I reside in Allentown, Pennsylvania.

Sixth Floor, Down the Hall and to the Left

I. Before the Lobotomy
On other walls, there are other pictures
of other people, not frozen in the city cold,
not barefoot on the chilling cement streets,
not crumbling like the buildings around them,
not in sorrow, not in war, and not bitter
for the life in their Man-destroyed world.
But where those pictures are, I do not know.

II. After the Lobotomy
Do I stare? I hadn't noticed.
What is it that mesmerizes me?
Is it the blank, blackened
frowns, the unshaven face, the
bones wrapped in dying skin, or
the eyes that remind me of me,
that the doctors tell me is something
good now? Please take the mirror
away; it reflects the sun at
noon and hurts my eyes, or
place it on another wall.

Michael Andrew Kingcaid

Artist's Profile
Vivian Wenhuey Chen
Andover, MA, USA

This poem etches the childhood of me and my three sisters. It calls back very dear memories. It also reflects that simple joys and the closeness of children can be fostered even under very poor material conditions.

Childhood

We grew up in Taipei in post-World War years
My sister and I
We sewed our own rag dolls
And we made our own toys

Our star-fruit tree house had no roof or floors
My sister and I
Selling fruits and buying flowers
We perched each on a branch the whole time

We had no rocking horses
My sister and I
Each had a bamboo stick
They got us places just fine

We also conducted big business
My sister and I
We took turns being president of our transportation enterprise
Collecting junk paper tickets from those who down the stair rails did slide

Vivian Wenhuey Chen

Dreams

I make the Z's somehow
nothing like the little one's work
Proper her scribbles run
from the first to the third lines
with first-grade ingenuity

She laughs at morning
from a night's play
of honky-tonk picking
at my nose and ears
singing songs of my ferocious inscriptions
upon the night's air

But no rainbow shined over my slumber
Only the yard bell hides the ghost
and I hurry to its calling

Yet she tells me of she and I
by a dirty pond filled with minnows
and asks what does it all mean
I stare into the light of the long day
but can't remember writing a single Z

Edgar Mixon

Thrift Shop Tabloids

La muse noir
prisoner de l'amour
I am the crisp, white petals
undaunted, unembarrassed handiwork
gathered bodice penning careful little notes
with sweet, scattered smudges.
Eliza danced in the springtime
but withered at the first snow
desperate, dreaming of marigolds
and lilac kisses.
Together we searched through fields of gold
for the promise hidden beneath the dirt.
In January winds we uncovered a path.
I found a nifty rock
speckled with silver stars
Eliza found Joseph.

We don't go digging anymore.

Amanda J. Mooney

Artist's Profile
Joseph Edsel Edmunds
Rockville, MD, USA

I'm a scientist who received a B.A. from the university of Puerto Rico, and an M.S. and Ph.D. from Cornell University in plant pathology and nematology, respectively. I'm a former ambassador of St. Lucia to the United Nations, Organization of American States, and the U.S. I'm an artist and poet. Some describe me as a Caribbean Renaissance man. The poem "Driftwood" is a manifestation of the transformation of an inanimate being through various influences and encounters into a thing of beauty produced by the Creator with the embellishment by an artist.

Driftwood

I found you at the river's mouth
On marshy ground, confronting the sea,
Soon to be engulfed by overpowering currents.
I captured you from impending oblivion,
For you preached a sermon of life
From burnt realities of rural imperatives
Slaughtered by cutlass and axe,
Severed from your rooted habitat.
From your once-serene mountaintop far away,
You escaped the final charcoal of energy.
You survived the rivers in transition,
Beautifully mutilated by streams and objects.
Your substance, with every encounter, changed
While you unconsciously assumed a form:
A being, unique, unparalleled, and singular.
I captured your essence and embraced
What only your creator could mold;
For I embellished your nature,
Transformed you into what you now are.
What a beautiful transfiguration.

Joseph Edsel Edmunds

Awaiting Spring

Darkness and dreams,
the winter that I hate
so much, and never realize
the bare trees like clawing
knuckles eroded from the
earth of a shallow grave—
clawing, clawing, clawing—
the unmoved isolation
of the sky.
I know the feeling, that sky feeling;
the gentle, endless rolling gray,
the joylessness of a rain
that must be given—a cold rain—
for days.
The crocuses were fooled
as were the azaleas; I wonder
if the sky breaks its awareness
out of the gray and rolling clouds
long enough to take a joyless glee
in frosting those early buds.

William B. Crenshaw

Colby, Kansas

I never knew light could fall this way
on a county

on such a done county and on such
done lives

but the flatlands do have their way
of rising up ruby from the ash and the dust

they have their way

of pulling from some
deep sweet nothing
a pocket full of splendors and

the malt they distend into fireworks.

You know, like a movie;
a trickle somewhere in the dawn

a flint of red across the sky
for one good second

a napalm drop

with the Cutlass humming by the side of the road
and the radio off

and your wedding band

and a tin heart.

Shannon Robert Mante

Artist's Profile
Cristen Burr Johnson
Virginia Beach, VA, USA

Emotion is the prevailing westerly that guides my 23-year-old psyche on an eternal quest to solidify my fluid realizations in a realm of time-less, natural beauty. I am a college student and work part-time. I enjoy writing, singing, and dancing. I would like to thank Kevin for encouraging me to pursue my dream of publishing my work. Without his support, my poems would only have the potential to take up mem-ory on my computer.

Emotional Atrophy

The dullness is there in my eyes
The luster of innocence replaced
With a filmy, distrustful cataract
Blinding me, binding me . . .

To a distorted, corroded funhouse, mirrored misinterpretation
A nauseating reflection
Of uncertainty and sheer irony
Devilishly dancing translucently
On the masculine roulette boards . . .

Where every empty male entity
Pried trust, forgiveness, and warmth
From the pristine pink of my complexion
With the manipulating forceps of love . . .

Cristen Burr Johnson

Artist's Profile
Jason Smith
Vancleve, KY, USA

The poem that I chose for this book was written in honor of my wife. I believe that if we honor God with our lives, and obey Him, no matter what the situation, He will honor us with the things that will complement us best. For me, that is my wife. She is all that I want or need in a wife. I consider her a true gift from God. I thank the Lord, Jesus Christ, for the way He has continuously challenged and encouraged me with her tender love.

My Enrapturing, Yet Constant Love

Warm, gentle breezes
Brush across the prairie
Soft, subtle scenes
Captured in moonlit sky
A serenade to serenity

Wondrous, rhythmic singing
Aboard the glowing ship
Graceful, peaceful, person
Dances with the stream
An enchanted, timeless trip

One bond, one love, one day
For time to weave its web
No deluded destiny
To hover in despair
A patient, passing ebb

Jason Smith

For Brian

Salty waves appear and dissipate,
One malignantly drenched in misery,
As a wretched valiant hovers
Unequivocally walking on water,
Rope in hand, heart in hand,
Aimed to ripple the pristine looking
Glass of snakes who lurch beneath
And desecrate stonewalled,
White picket fences.
Open casket earned pleasantries
Condolences on clichéd breath with
Cliched salutations. Glaring eyeteeth
Suck clean the rusted carnations
And pupils cackle vehemently, mercilessly
As sirens hum incessantly, lullaby,
Rock-a-bye of soothing apathy.
Somewhere south of persistence
A coiled canvas of good intentions
Shivers under hunter's warmth.

Christina Griffin Santucci

Untitled

questions tumble
out of answers
late at night
like socks
from a coin slot dryer
at an all-night laundromat,
half-in, half-out
when the door opens,
still damp and balled
or hanging
from the roof
of the hot tin cave
like a bat.

why, for example.

Carol L. Ayres

Artist's Profile
Nancy L. Marier
Island Pond, VT, USA

I was born and raised in the great north woods of New Hampshire. I started writing poetry at Franconia College in Franconia, New Hampshire. I put writing aside to raise my family, and serve my community in 4-H Club, Veterans of Foreign Wars, and as a town employee. Between my son and daughter, I have five grandchildren. "Our Cradled Hearts" was penned describing Richard E. Isbell of Alabama. He is my best friend, lover, confidant, cowboy, and every mate I've needed and wanted. I am now divorced, and full of anticipation for our pending marriage.

Our Cradled Hearts

Absence cannot box our passion,
Ingredients, love's chemistry all.
Purest beauty, humor, sincerity,
Sent cradled hearts delivered to
Our frosty bosoms flurries' songs.
Our breaths and hands are held,
Awe of the golden gifts and music.
Our souls, our love meets and will
'Til the mountains become that one
Last grain of sand and the waters,
All water on Earth, is reduced to
Eight ounces, and we share that drink as
The stars, the moon, and the sun
Reveal their secrets.

Nancy L. Marier

Conformity Is a Fallacy

Conformity is the great fallacy,
Which screams thy word to silence of thy name,
And places rest to final destiny,
To touch with hands discerned by scorching flame.
'Tis fair to blame the preachers for the dead,
When darkness falls upon her purple grace,
'Tis fair to blame what rulers had once said,
When golden cloths do hide her wicked face.
She does not give, she does not take, do mind,
Yet sits entangled, vines of utter fate,
As poison beauty makes the venom blind,
I force her to release the love and hate.
They differ from the other's hazel eyes,
Conform, do dream, in Satan's bed of lies.

Devon Garrett Dickau

Superstition Mountain

Climbing over Superstition Mountain,
I find I cannot be left standing
among the family bones,
frank, brittle, and unbending,
not a Dixie rebel yell or North Side curse
left there among this family
you and I never had.
You, borrowed velour stuck
tangled up in blue,
warmer and wetter than
the red rock pushing forward
to me out of the
communes and car parts, snow and forests
of Jerome behind.
I am too young to drive the roads
where the desert moon is rising,
too bright for me to bury you by,
in the land where I lost what we never had,
where the mesquite-sage air smells
like your newfound smoker's breath.

Ilissa Michelle Gould

Artist's Profile

Edgardo Adriano de Lara

Dallas, TX, USA

Texas is bigger than life for me. Growing up in a tropical country like the Philippines vastly changed my perspective on how things are in other parts of the world. I have adopted Texas and its people as my own, my second home!

Texas

Soaring mass of billowing clouds,
a dusty wall from New Mexico
heralds another front; hovering,
hesitating,
in the end trapping,
there it is concluding our summer ordeal
for the moment.

Thunderstorms can be like that,
as a native Texan loves his own weather
as beloved as prickly pear;
where else in God's land
can this wondrous landscape be carved,
using flash floods to sculpt
and polish with howling winds
to test His own people
thus, this land is yours for the moment.

Edgardo Adriano de Lara

Paria Canyon

I stand
in powdered chocolate, offerings
from the sandstone gods, all here
in profile, breathing shafts
of light—epiphanies—that
shine through shadowed passages
of time;

Undo my vest, take in the cool—
a poultice for what aches inside.

Walk on
and leave my print until
next boot obscures, next
flood obliterates;

Leave only
spirit purified,
distilled by place and time,
to what is basic and
unknowable.

Susan Marie Benson

Racing

Riding the wind,
wide-eyed, surfing
the light in darkness,
mechanically suppressing the urge
to throw the head backwards,
to become one
with the breathing.

Tempting distance,
a speeding flip of intimacy,
searching arms flung eagerly
around me, craving
for completion.
We,
the living rocket
once calmly released,
breaking irresistibly
through barrages at the boarder,
compass needles whirling
through a black magnetic field.

Chris Wanten

Artist's Profile
Michelle G. Stradford
Westchester, OH, USA

I am in love with words. I am inspired and strengthened and torn down by words. I am comforted by the rhythm of syllables and vowels. I am revealed by words. My words are the most precious gift that God has granted me, for through them I touch and share and hope and remember. Words make my ordinary daily existence an extraordinary experience. I am a mother, wife, daughter, sister, and friend who is also an architect, a dabbling artist, and an aspiring writer. Poetry and writing is the mirror through which I dare to peer into my soul.

Blue Sanctum

I hold my hand for a long moment
Under the warm rush of water
As rising steam slowly fills the room
Flushing my face

Beaming in the yellow warmth that surrounds me
One by one, I light flames that flicker
Excitedly in anticipation
As lavender oil free-falls from the crystal blue vase
I hold high above the white claw-foot tub
Where purple puddles gather atop the water
Awaiting the commencement

My weary feet carry me across the cool tile floor
Where I close the door and catch the lock
And listen to quiet
Soft saxophone notes waft through tiny crevices
Taming my ragged mind, inducing calm

Finally, I immerse my being into the blue sanctum
Devoid of today, of tomorrow, of self
I close my eyes and see clearly
And soak it all in, filling up until I am renewed again

Michelle G. Stradford

Tales of Land and Steed

I have never seen the horses
Of Sable Island,
The fabled beasts of the sand.
They are not creatures named
And tamed by masters rude,
Instead nurtured by sea breeze wild,
Vividly alive on bare naked land.

The drunken horses of Bamiyan
Pray not the Arabian stallion
(You might have heard)
Are veiled and curtailed
Many times over by bearded
Men of God, fueled
By an ardor to force
Paradise to ground.

Remember Pegasus,
The myth that travels
Faster than the light,
Remains our peerless shining light.

Elzy Taramangalam

Ascension

It's been a while since I felt the harsh grain of our
Gate swing inward, beckoning me forward to enter
The house that was my home. Images of a dauphin hour
Filling the room and glimmering like a dream in the mirror.
Time bends back again, accompanying my slow pace.
Each step, a year; each stair, eternal. Polished frames show
The childish delight of all things precious, lost in the race
For money, pride, and glory. A trick for fate to bestow.
The creaks of the body blend with those of my path, an
Echo eternal, bespeaks silence once filled with golden joy.
Early life, a shade of a shadow, the river sorrow overran.
Memories and dreams beckoned with a blink, destroyed.
The vision strengthens, and I straighten on the landing,
A traveller finding his path, his purpose, his song,
The past now left behind. Such a narrow corridor to bring
Redemption. The first breath, my last, a new life to sing.

Scott Anthony Nodwell

Check-Out

I sit on my bags here at the station.
I've toured the city, exchanged my currency,
now there's nothing left to do here but wait.
The news greets me with relief.
I made it back to the station.
I could just as easily have been ruined
in riches or wretchedness.
My passport awaits its stamp
certifying my time here—
time earned, time wasted, time lost.
I won't miss my time here, though many
I have loved, and almost felt my heart belonged there.
But there lies a secret land far greater,
which rings and embraces the tawdry city.
My ears attuned to the call of the forest.
My nose filled with the smell of sweet rain.
My hands find their home again
in this sweet earth.
My body belonged to you all along.

William Michael Kallfelz

Marc 1

Marc, I still love and miss you.

I like you
just because you never leave me
alone in soliloquy
in the silent orange and translucent dark
sitting, because we're both too tired to stand
and vulnerable
breathing deep, lucid smoke
and not caring when it's suddenly jade
but the warmth never leaves me
like it probably rubs off you
and you can feel my coated skin
dripping off everything you say
but you lead me
and I'm in an illuminated, normal
forest of sapphire instead of juniper
and breezy
as your voice echoes through jealous canyons
towering all that was my life

Sheila Gertrude Nofchissey

Beneath a Rainbow Robe

The things I cannot say to you
Wrench around in my throat
Like a mechanical wheel fallen off its track.
They flit to the tip of my dry tongue
And flirt with disaster
Only to trickle back inside my lips
And cascade down to the bellowing black below.

The things I cannot say to you
Hold my heart inside a cell;
Walls that close in and out,
In and out with methodical rhythms,
Tortuous songs that echo the same few words.

The things I cannot say to you
Blind my petty reason and ring in my ears,
Resonate with passion,
Flow into a fury that only I can feel;
And oh, do I feel
My secret love.

Marissa Savastana

That Morning in London Town

Grimy, soot-ridden rags
sit between the day's rations and the
battered wireless in the corner.
Somehow the voice was much clearer.
Eighth of May, '45, proclaimed "The Times."
Left the house early that foggy morning,
walked past rows of destroyed houses, rows
of shattered dreams and murdered hopes.
But red, red blossoms had bloomed
as blood gushing from the maimed earth.
I realized then
that it was spring.
And as we walked on, walked on,
we heard the voices of a great multitude,
a rising crescendo of hope, love, and
triumph, and lo!
As the larks soared overhead on the wings of
the dawn, it seemed as though the darkness
fled before them.

Julian Matius Tagal

together alone

strangers together and so far apart
they stay together—they make it an art

what turns people into strangers i don't know
i guess they're in limbo, together alone

make love together without getting close
or trying to uncover what they need most

what turns lovers into strangers i don't know
i guess they're just people together alone

they stay together, but they know it's a lie
they stay together, never quite knowing why

what turns lovers into liars i don't know
i guess they're just people

together alone.

Stephanie Cobb Lau

James Dean

I am sitting alone at midnight
Beneath a lamppost in the embrace of a tree
James Dean is haunting this street.
The lamppost is lonely, it strikes midnight with every breath,
Its shadow falls across me; I am the five o'clock morning, I am death,
James Dean is haunting this street.
You said "Grace is submission," you said I needed love,
You sat beautiful and talked about loneliness, you sat
Faithful and talked about belief.
Well, if I wanted a river, I could find one right now,
But I don't want annihilation, I just want sympathy.
I want you to find me, alone at midnight,
With James Dean haunting this street.

Hannah Jennifer Emily Wilks

The One-Year Mark

A girl who is made of sky
remains in my thoughts
as a telling sign
Somewhere she had grown as a lilac rose,
a Celeste; rambling, tall and strong
Today she runs through the field,
a red flame on a June evening
her curly hair straight, her covered legs bare
and her intellect raging
Her disdain for me, tousled and unsure, yet
twisting my heart in awkward directions
A year passed since the promises I made
about her and still regret pulsates with
the flies around my head
I love her and her not me
I split apart and swiftly she places her
hand in the wound
And now, as I pass from heaven back to the
dirty ground
I see only her face and don't want to leave

Rebecca Cobby

Treasure Hunt

Just because you don't see the sun,
my friend, does not mean it isn't there.
Poke your head above the dark clouds,
you'll find its glory shining there.

When it seems hope is no longer yours,
a lost and missing commodity, long gone,
look out and see the ever-newborn day,
as it stretches its wings with the dawn.

The best treasures call for a little searching
before they yield themselves, it's true.
Get a bigger shovel, look hard as you can,
for happiness is a chosen gift meant for you.

When gloom hangs low, get a broom
and sweep every black inch out and away.
Sounds easy, but it isn't, it's difficult,
and sometimes those clouds want to stay.

This is your day, hours to live life free,
to explore the possibilities you will find.
Gather up sunshine and love, my friend,
power is right there, in your very own mind.

Sherry Asbury

Doha, Qatar

High wind from the Gulf tonight,
dust sandbagging the sky; the sun
still roseate on high thunderclouds
and the trees, trembling. A scene
uncommon as clay in this wilderness
and one promising summer rain. The air,
charged with expectation, reeks,
and wave on wave washes in the war.
Lightning licks;
clouds are lit, low and black and elegant;
near, too near. Dry lightning, dry wind,
dry rain falling upward to darkness again.

John Stephen Morris

lemonade

in summer we speak
soft tones as the heat
drinks our sweat
faster than we can sip
our lemonade

standing on street corners
wild whispers so she can hear
pretend though
silence is golden as giggles
our glances

meet and moments
stretch like a barnyard cat
tingle like midnight movies
touch the seams of passion
and match the searing sun

glasses hide but in you i can feel
soft tones as the heat
drinks our sweat
faster than we can sip
our lemonade

Kristine Hayden Schubert

Artist's Profile
Robert W. Alexander
Davis, CA, USA

My poem is the result of the overpowering beauty of living many summers in Italy, overlooking the Gulf of Policastro, the ancient Greek "Sinus Lao." Living in such natural beauty finally resulted in my designing and making the sculpture I name "Awe." Placed on a tile terrace, it faces continually the view that grew within me; it gazes south toward Sicily, awaiting another full moon, when terraces fill and footsteps hesitate by serpentine walls.

"Awe Del Mondo"

Entrapped, Awe stands,
In beauty's grasp, gazing at the
Rhythmic beating of an ancient sea.
Upon the grander stoic promontories,
Stretching high, causing
Drifting dreams to often cry.

Gira, gira, gira
For night is before day,
Then day before night.

Gira, gira, gira
Moon before sun and soon
Sun before another moon.

Gira, gira, gira
Once again over "Sinus Lao"
Shedding its shimmering light
Stealing darkness from night.

Robert W. Alexander

Shake of the Head

And I have been waiting to open the lies
Slowly tear away the paper of the envelope
And expose everything
So that it may spray out in excitement
Take everyone for a sucker
Or perhaps just another piece
On the game board, spinning 'round
It needs me like a society needs its soil
At least something needs me
Because the eyes cast away
As my head has never found a comfortable
And balanced position
Above plain concrete my soles are stuck to
Everyone's around the table
Anxious, with their eyes locked on the letter
And everyone leaves the table
Once the letter slips into my pocket
Curiosity is just so contagious
But no one cares to say hello
To something or someone they already know

Jeremy Steven Fizette

Autumn Shadows

Leaves press against the window.
The door opens and closes slightly, breathing
in the afternoon.
Something unknown drags itself across the
carpet, appears to exist more so than I.

There is one and one who is not.
There cannot be one without the other.
This truth begins with conceiving and bearing
its being both, made alive through my own
breathing.

I am never alone.

Mark Brennan

Columbia

First day
of the second month
of the third year.

Aligned:
Seven swans' migration
and backwing to Earth nest.

Crowd's collective eye stings

from the sun of eighty-six,
from the sun of now;

waiting, wild for
its flock to alight.

A fire.
Moon's dark regard.

Toward neither space
nor sky
seven swans glide on
star surface,
bury bitter beak in white wing

and never return.

Amy Wink Krebs

Moonlight

The saltwater-covered sand,
beneath the ebb and flow of cold,
groping waves, rolls away,
leaving bare, lost pieces of the sea, dead
jellyfish, and bleached driftwood.

I dial the seven numbers you scribbled
carelessly onto a matchbook cover
after we languished until sunset
in the backroom at the Blue Lagoon
where even shadows could leave you longing.

With you on the line my thoughts recede.
Words move gradually into the distance
until our conversation fills with bones.

A web of darkness cloaks the sea,
a cerulean moon hovers over foreboding dunes.
After a conversation disrobed by silence,
you hang up.
The sound of your goodbye hits me like a
sudden August downpour.

Teri Ann Whittington

Postcard from Mexico

After a week of rain, your card arrived,
but not the sun. I read it still soaked;
some of the writing bled. Here, towels and jeans
never quite dry, and black water swells the gutters.

Caught in the cold rain, the city is helpless;
drowned worms thread the sidewalks.
All night, cars hiss on the streets.
I dream of you, brown on white sand.

Out walking, feet wet, I pause
in the scented warmth rising from a Laundromat.
Where you are, white walls hold the long day's heat
and careless flowers leaven the night air.

Alice N. Persons

Drifting

Ten inches of new snow
shape-shifts, erases
the thin blue line between earth and sky.
An unending undulation
envelops the sound of footsteps,
of passing vehicles, of cold.
I break the drifts
in gloved hands and green Sorels.
The metal shovel scrapes across cement—
pierces the quiet, quiet hush.
I feel my nostrils sting.
I see the shimmering, sub-zero sky
spin around the sun,
watch the glitter fall from frozen air,
witness the wave of white's
ascension into Heaven.
In this small moment, I know
how it must feel
to breathe.

A. B. Smith

breeze

even now my fair companion
a pretty young breeze perfumed with summer
plays gently and dances in plum
and the words of a poet and laughing
like water she kisses my cheek
like fingers of sun
and ripples the pond and tripping with reason
she raises the frills of her song
now trumpets of geese
and the waving of clover
coax modesty from her
and blushing she belts out her tune
absconding my breath
for her finale with blossoms
of amber and june
she bows and she leaves me
like a toy from my childhood
like a drink at the tavern
spinning and stirring
and begging for more

Michael P. Roy

Feral Child

Frolicking amongst sensuous daisies,
self-consciously aware, she darts,
impatiently, gathering petals and scents,
her skin gleaming and essential.

Like a scared rabbit she flees,
requiring my gaze, each leap nearing my
sacred boundary of maternal patience, seeking
to ignite that indulgent flame of pity and
impetuous love, buried somewhere deep.

Her soft eyes demand Demeter's affection,
penetrating beyond my casual pretense
and stolid facade—I watch her endlessly
until one day she obliterates the rules
of my fortress, proud defense powerless
against a fleet of mountainous emotions.

Though my frail arms cannot contain her
feral spirit, just once, by the lamppost,
next to the daisy field, I will catch her,
and as I hold her she will know
she is beautiful.

Kristina Erika Foltz

untitled

broken tokens
words unspoken
dreams lie broken
to die. to die.
death becomes her.
life, a huge blur
wafting like feathers
lighter than air.
breathing, bleeding
pleading
needing
conceding
eternally.

Nichole Marie Duban

"Tasogare"

Lurid dreaming,
cast upon cinnamon-swirled
featureless dusk
Afterglow of an ember robust
drapes softly
the twilight indigo
into quiet nooks
of velvet memory
As pizzicato bursts of static
intermesh the Philomel
to mark with punctuation
a metronome's progression
The soft lit cascading
celestial illumination
an ivory comb rests
in the shimmering
ebony tresses
of a lover returned

Robert M. Lane

Artist's Profile
Amy Ehn
Seattle, WA, USA

Words are the building blocks of language. Language has the potential to bring together nations. Words can create understanding, which then might lead to compassion, a sense of unification based solely on the shared reactions to these words. Regardless of what color your skin is, where you live, who you love, or even when you were born, we all have dreams. Indeed, actualizing these is simply a matter of believing in yourself. Thanks, Dad!

5:43 A.M.

In the soft hush of the early morning light,
I catch a fleeting glimpse of a dream weaver
Sneaking away with the first crisp rays of the rising sun.
I smell the scent of sleep she leaves behind,
Clinging desperately to my lover's skin.
Golden and damp,
Warm and sultry,
The night visions, their mysteries, the quiet of dawn.
These too will soon be gone.
I caress the unruly locks of his hair,
Touch my ruby red lips to his rosy cheek,
Run my cool fingers over the nape of his neck.
I inhale deeply and there it is again,
Intoxicating and inviting,
Like the scent of nothing else I know.
It pulls me in, wraps its arms around me.
And through my soul
Plunging into the vast eternal bliss of my existence,
Saturating the very fibers of my being,
I am bathed in the aroma of his dreams.

Amy Ehn

The Wild West

Remember when the West had shootouts, and brawls
So rough and ready, still the church bell rung
As country gents drew a gun made law and order
Bankers, blacksmiths, women folk were among
Posted rewards across the border
When gunslingers set foot in the West to decay
Loot and rob were crimes that fetched the outlaw's desire
The duty of the good guy sheriff is to gun down its prey
As cowboys saddled up in western attire
Word reached the people deserting the town
Gun duels to settle was for one to expire
Saloons, banks, and stores were quickly shut down
Just the outlaw and sheriff made eye contact alone
With the stroke of high noon set the burning hot sun
The two in duel fired bullets like pellets of stone
As the skill of the sheriff's quick gun stood one
Winning the girl ended with the outlaw dead on the ground
Law and order was brought to the western small town
With the motto "Have Gun Will Travel" saloon bound
Starring Western heroes in a story legend handed down

Cheryl Pinckney

Something Out There

Passing through life, a sudden hint
Perhaps a memory or a glimpse; is it?
Something out there.
Is it or is it not; perhaps or perhaps not;
Something out there. A shadow of what may
Come; such unforeseen that once begun . . .
Frozen in my steps, just a memory or a
Glimpse, was it or was it not . . . something
Out there?
In flight of wings, ever present, hiding in
Or hiding out . . . is something out there; oh,
Treasure light of unforeseen, that which is
Revealed behind a scene . . . do we understand
A treasure of what is out there?

April Lee Strouse

Past Tense

The past is
a song sung
in a foreign language.
You recognize some
things by inflection,
intuition. Your eyes smile,
crescent moons in a knowing sky.
You walk alone on a beach,
each step a gritty samba to
a tune
unnamed. You turn,
step back
into the tracks you left
in the sand.
You end at the beginning.
A seagull
heralds your arrival,
on wings fully spread.

Rose Maria Woodson

Life of Siddhartha

A young Brahmin boy was standing under
The light of sun that was very bright
For he was young and his heart had thunder
To explore his inner self was his fight
He wanted to meet his inner soul
He did not want himself to be deceived
He went to change his life as a whole
He had many goals to be achieved
A stop in the way was garden of pleasure
Buddha's teachings were also insightful
Garden was tempting but not a treasure
Teachings to him were not delightful
He was mentor he needed no teacher
He found his atmaan in a river

Muhammad Qadeer

Colorado Twilight

First, the Indian quiet.
No elk or buffalo around,
no rumor of thunder, pledge of rain,
in the slow August air.
The birds agree.
Points of late sun
mark leaves from another season,
bark underfoot a thousand years.

Let the aspen stand fast.
High against amaretto sky,
I saddle sudden wind to a higher place
where the stars squint,
and in my eyes, new moon,
sketched low to the mountain
at the gathering dark,
coyote trail silent in night smells,
an owl, one eye open, imagines sleep.

Lee L. Berkson

Joined of Absence

Joined by a stranger
dressed in street clothes,
yellow dome lights blink,
the southern city slowly being rewritten
and faint with fog.
Absent for many years,
he sits, faceless, towards the curses
of the East.
Blades don't turn fast enough;
mirrors don't distort enough;
whispers don't bend enough.
Joined by a stranger
sweeping bits of glassy commons
into the keys
of a typewriter,
the unearthly mist seeps on. . . .

Valerie Rose Byxbe

Artist's Profile
Allison Mitcham
Sumner, IA, USA

A number of my poems that readers have responded to most warmly have—like this one—had to do with gardens and gardening in relation to human behavior and emotions. Of the twenty five books I have published to date, four have been poetry books. Some emotions and insights, I find, just don't lend themselves to prose so well as poetry. In poetry, certain truths, as the poet sees them, have to be briefly encapsulated. And yes, truth to tell, I am a devoted gardener!

A Huge Leap of Faith

It is still early February
and until the seed catalogues began arriving,
I wasn't sure I could survive the winter.

Even then,
I was slow to respond
to the vibrant images
of lettuce and sunflowers,
petunias and broccoli,
strawberries and blackberries.

Their seemingly too-ripe promises
of flowers and fruitfulness
held me back,
while at the same time urging me to commit myself
to make a huge leap of faith,
to believe, despite visible signs to the contrary,
that spring and summer are in the offing.
That I will still be here
to plant the proffered seed,
to reap the promised crop.

Allison Mitcham

Artist's Profile
Anna Malone
Tuscumbia, AL, USA

After my mother had survived triple bypass surgery and the removal of a brain tumor the following year, my family and I realized that she was no longer "Mama." I wrote "My Favorite Color Is Red" in honor of my mother. I have tried to be the kind of mother to my three children that my mother was to me. Family is very important to me. I'm blessed to have a close, loving family. Poetry is a wonderful way for me to express my feelings about my family, as well as other important events in my life.

My Favorite Color Is Red

You told me I was stubborn, waiting three days for my arrival.
Yet you kissed my skinned knees and held me close long, dark nights.
You made for me Easter dresses, pink and blue,
And gave me pennies for the rolling candy store.
We went for walks in the woods,
Shuffling through the leaves eating muscadines.
Together we went shopping at Elmore's Five and Dime
And shared our favorite books.
You were always there when I needed you—
Graduation, wedding, and each child's birth.
Three times you came and stayed at my home, helping me to adjust.
And when my true love left, you said, "All things work for the best.
Take one day at a time."
Now times are different. Everything has changed.
You've always known me so well, but now . . .
You can't remember that
My favorite color is red.

Anna Malone

Preparation

I watch you spark peach to plum in the
clearing we move toward.
Winter knocks on our ribs and feet as we
hunt a tree to dress for Christmas by
drinking nearly frozen Vodka and hanging
salt dough ornaments.

The wind calls snow for you, bangs the
ladder as you hang the lights out front.
There is a smoke to your smile; a gray
smirky tone that makes me always want to say yes to my falling.

The ash of our conversation forms a single
ridge on the surface of our life.
It spirals back onto us forming a crest of
time like cartilage fusing flesh to bone.
You flame the lamps, hoping not to let go
the light that changes our table's linen.

Mark Brennan